101
Easy Asian
Recipes

Lucky Peach

Presents

101
Easy
Asian
Recipes

Peter Meehan
and the editors of *Lucky Peach*

Clarkson Potter/Publishers
NEW YORK

Peter Meehan, editorial director
Mary-Frances Heck, recipe development
Gabriele Stabile, photography
Mark Ibold, food styling & male hand modeling
Hannah Clark, prop styling
Joanna Sciarrino, managing editor
Rica Allannic, Rachel Khong, Brette Warshaw, Chris Ying, editors
Walter Green & Helen Tseng, design and layout
Jason Polan, illustrations
Kate Slate, copy editor
Ena Brdjanovic & Sai Sumar, interns
Special thanks to: Danny Bowien, Dave Chang, Joanne Chang,
Angela Dimayuga, Fuschsia Dunlop, Tony Kim, Miki Takana,
Regina Kwan Peterson, Andy Ricker, Laurie Woolever, Bary Yuen

Published in the United States by Clarkson Potter/Publishers, an
imprint of the Crown Publishing Group, a division of
Penguin Random House, LLC, New York.
www.crownpublishing.com
www.clarksonpotter.com

CLARKSON POTTER is a trademark and POTTER with colophon
is a registered trademark of Penguin Random House, LLC.

Hot and Sour Soup (page 110) adapted from Joanne Chang's
*Flour, Too: Indispensable Recipes for the Café's Most-Loved
Sweets & Savories* (Chronicle Books, 2013).

Library of Congress Cataloging-in-Publication Data
Meehan, Peter, 1977– author.
Lucky Peach 101 easy Asian recipes / Peter Meehan and the
editors of Lucky Peach; Photographs by Gabriele Stabile.—First
Edition.
pages cm
Includes index.
1. Cooking, Asian. I. Lucky peach. II. Title.
TX724.5.A1M44 2015
641.595—dc23   2015015729

ISBN 978-0-8041-8779-4
Ebook ISBN 978-0-8041-8790-9

Printed in China

Book and cover design by Walter Green

10 9 8 7 6 5 4 3 2 1

First Edition

For Big H, Little H, and Joni-Bird

Contents

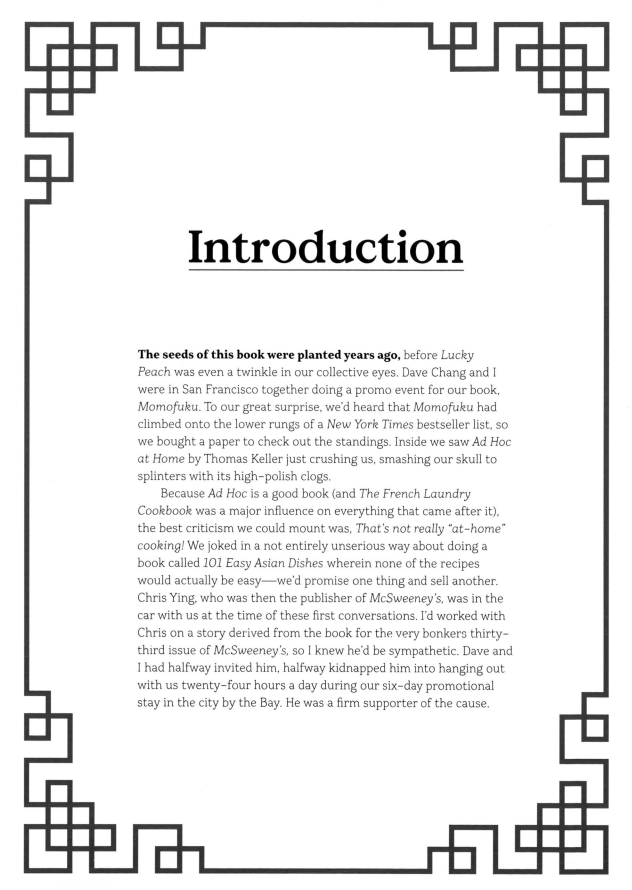

Introduction

The seeds of this book were planted years ago, before *Lucky Peach* was even a twinkle in our collective eyes. Dave Chang and I were in San Francisco together doing a promo event for our book, *Momofuku*. To our great surprise, we'd heard that *Momofuku* had climbed onto the lower rungs of a *New York Times* bestseller list, so we bought a paper to check out the standings. Inside we saw *Ad Hoc at Home* by Thomas Keller just crushing us, smashing our skull to splinters with its high-polish clogs.

Because *Ad Hoc* is a good book (and *The French Laundry Cookbook* was a major influence on everything that came after it), the best criticism we could mount was, *That's not really "at-home" cooking!* We joked in a not entirely unserious way about doing a book called *101 Easy Asian Dishes* wherein none of the recipes would actually be easy—we'd promise one thing and sell another. Chris Ying, who was then the publisher of *McSweeney's*, was in the car with us at the time of these first conversations. I'd worked with Chris on a story derived from the book for the very bonkers thirty-third issue of *McSweeney's,* so I knew he'd be sympathetic. Dave and I had halfway invited him, halfway kidnapped him into hanging out with us twenty-four hours a day during our six-day promotional stay in the city by the Bay. He was a firm supporter of the cause.

Back in New York I got to work on it. I remember setting pineapple juice with agar agar inside jalapeños, then slicing the results so a ring of fiery green would encircle a disk of cool sweet yellow fruit jelly. These were going to go on a Hawaiian pizza (Hawaii being more or less part of Asia the way we were counting it).

But then we started this TV show project that became *The Mind of a Chef* and begat our magazine, *Lucky Peach*, and then that became the beast that swallowed my life. Ying was no longer an innocent and enthusiastic bystander, but a collaborator and eventually my partner in crime in running the operation.

When the roller coaster of launching the magazine hit a flat patch—or, really, when we acclimatized to its speed, because it hasn't slowed down at all—it was time to think: What's the first *Lucky Peach* book going to be? I pushed for it to be that primordial version of *101* at the outset, but it quickly felt wrong. For one thing, we now had a magazine in which we could air our craziest dirty-idea laundry, and we'd regularly done that—publishing insanely complicated recipes was part of our 9-to-5 gig. Plus I'd had two kids in the interim and reconnected with the beauty and, more essentially, the necessity of good and easy ways to get dinner on the table.

And so *101*, which had always been a joke, morphed into an earnest thing, a project where we could publish simple and flavorful recipes with the home cook in mind. Most food magazines start out with that goal; for us, it was a new challenge. And the results of taking on that challenge are what you hold in your hands.

At the outset, I set forth two rules to hem us in:

1. No Frying

Frying isn't hard in the least, but it makes a mess, and if you cook at all at home, you know that cleaning up is half the battle. I'm sure we'll do a book of all fried foods at some point to make up for the restraint exercised here.

2. No Subrecipes

This turned out to be a rule that had to be broken, because no matter how easy you make things, sometimes cooking requires additional cooking. But we kept it to a minimum and tried to be honest about it. We avoided anything like, "Make this meal in ten minutes as long as you spend a whole day the week before cooking a jar of goop that you'll never actually use for anything else!" (There is a small chapter of flavorful goops toward the back of the book that you *will* use frequently. They're our go-to Super Sauces that can be dumped over nearly any food lingering in your fridge to turn it into delicious dinners.)

As far as what we mean by "easy," it's all about practical considerations. Some recipes might sit on your stove or in a slow-cooker for a couple hours, but that doesn't make them difficult. Some recipes, like the dumplings on pages 60 to 64, might require an hour of active kitchen work, but we don't expect those to be weeknight meals, and we figure the return more than justifies the investment of time.

Of course, many of the recipes in this book call for ingredients that you can't buy at the local gas station. But in the age of online grocery suppliers, even hermits can arrange for a delivery of a full pantry's worth of goods to their local trailhead and have 98 percent of the dishes contained herein on their table the next night. I personally find the thrill of physically seeking out these products in actual markets to be about as much fun and rewarding as most guys my age find fantasy sports, golf, or strip clubs, which is to say a lot. But to each his own. Just don't cry into your pillow about how you can't find them, because you can.

The last thing to address before we get on to the real show here is the "Asian" thing. We are acutely aware that Asia's size and complexity are so vast that it is a ridiculous idea to reduce its cuisines—each its own private infinity once you begin to parse regions and subregions and the variations and innovations that individual cooks employ in their kitchens every day—down to 101 recipes that are representative of anything. There's nothing from India in here, or Tajikistan for that matter; Cambodia gets short shrift too. If one thing has remained from the original idea for *101* it is our cavalier and labradoodle-enthusiastic approach to what we mean when we talk about Asia. Completeness is an impossibility, and not our goal.

We appreciate hyperspecific, traditional recipes that call for truly hard labor and criminally obscure ingredients as much as the next nerd; we and many of our friends often cook and write recipes in that vein. But we all work long hours and come home hungry to cold kitchens, or have kids to feed, or want to cook because, when days are chaotic, there is a restorative beauty to the order and purpose of cutting things up and turning them into sustenance. For whatever else you can't control, you can put dinner on the table. The recipes in this book are meant to be fuel for those moments, solutions to those situations.

So we chose favorite dishes and recipes that were naturally simple. We stripped down some things into reasonable facsimiles of their source material. Other recipes appear here because they're a funny part of the comically broad idea of what "Asian" cuisine encompasses for us, even though their genesis and diaspora are distinctly late-twentieth-century American.

Above all, we tried to have fun, and to put together a folio of kitchen ideas that you can turn to for easy eating on a real-life schedule and budget. Dig it, and dig in.

—Peter Meehan and the editors of *Lucky Peach*

Equipment

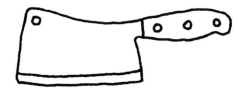

In making this book we really tried to whittle down the required equipment. The items you see here are things that made our experience of cooking this food better and easier. The two things you have to get: a **wok (1)** and a **rice cooker (2)**.

I'd advise springing for a rice cooker with a timer, so you can have it make fresh hot rice for you when you get up in the morning or get home from work at night. You certainly do not *need* a rice cooker to make rice—a pot, a faucet, and any primitive heat source will get the job done—but almost everybody I know from a rice-eating part of the world uses one, and since being converted, I do too. It's a worthwhile convenience: It's not more of a mess than a pot, and once you add the rice and the water (and any flavorings, should you go down that road), it's done, and you can focus on the rest of the meal.

Do not buy a nonstick wok or I will come to your house and beat you over the head with it. Go to a Chinatown if there's one near you, and do not spend more than $20. It should be thin but sturdy, made of steel, and flat-bottomed so it works on your stove. Most woks will come with instructions for how they should be seasoned; the short version is this: Wash well, heat over high heat, add a lot of fat, and stir-fry a bunch of chopped chives until they're completely hammered, about 10 minutes or so. Cool, rinse clean, and it's ready to use.

As far as the rest, a **wok spatula (3)** is a pleasurable tool for pushing food around a wok, which is something this book will ask you to do often. I honestly didn't own one— I'd always used flat wooden spoons—until we started pulling this collection together, and I won't do without one going forward. (Also, we started referring to it as a wok shovel, which just makes me like it more.)

The **spider (4)** is the slotted spoon of the Asian kitchen. It is worth more than the $3 it will cost you. The **mortar and pestle (5)** is a pain to haul home from the store, but it really does make certain things, particularly Thai things, taste right. You can absolutely do without one, but if you get into making curry pastes, you'll like owning one. Buy a fairly sizable model if you spring for one, one that holds at least 2 cups of stuff, so you can use it for dishes like the papaya salad on page 56.

Noodles

One could write a telephone book or two about Asian noodles and probably leave a lot out, so we'll avoid straying into that territory here. Any city/town/unincorporated municipality with a good Asian supermarket or two will have most of these, and the Internet has the rest. Fresh ramen and fresh rice noodles are the two hardest to come by on account of their freshness. But I recently came across vacuum-sealed packages of fresh rice noodles (marketed as Pad See Ew Noodles, which is, in fact, how we use them) at the local Whole Foods, and fresh ramen is slowly stretching its alkaline tendrils across America, thanks largely to (the excellent) Sun Noodle company.

Unless you're buying your noodles like loosies out of the back of a truck to keep costs down, everything will be sold with cooking instructions and times on their packaging. Follow them.

1. Ramen
Fresh ramen noodles are a world apart from the stuff in your cup of noodles, and are worth seeking out. They are toothsome in a manner different from, but recalling, fresh pasta, with a distinctive flavor that's the tiniest bit sulfurous in a very good way. If you can't find them and are some kind of type A overachieving person who's slumming it here in an easy cookbook, check our website— or the Internet in general if *Lucky Peach* has gone the way of the dodo—for a simple recipe to make them yourself.

2. Soba

Soba noodles are made with buckwheat, which lays claim to their distinctive flavor. Fresh soba is too delicate to be sold commercially in any scalable amounts, so you'll be cooking with dried. About this, be happy.

3. Udon

Udon, a thick wheat noodle from Japan, is kind of the workingman's noodle. Udon makers actually jump up and down on bags of the noodle dough to maximize the gluten, and the result is a hearty noodle that can stand up to hot broth or big flavors. They're not specifically called for in any recipes herein, but they'd go well with any of the ragus on pages 136 to 138 and the two ginger-scallion sauces (page 246), or as an alternative to somen or soba.

4. Lo mein

Lo mein are the size and shape of thick spaghetti and yellow from egg (not food coloring). We recommend cooking them for a minute or two to loosen them up, but letting them finish cooking in whatever stir-fry or broth situation you have going.

5. Rice noodles

The two main categories of rice noodles are fresh and dried. Fresh rice noodles can be delicate and fine or sturdy and stir-fryable. We call for them only once, in Pad See Ew (page 128), which is made with the fresh wide rice noodles called *sen yai*. Fresh rice noodles clump easily, and sometimes novice users (like me, once or twice) will try to boil them to get the noodles separated. Word to the wise: That cooks them into a lump. Instead, peel them apart in a colander under cold running water—there will be winners and losers in the process, not everybody comes out whole—and then use as directed, with a hot wok.

Dried rice noodles are a staple of Southeast Asian cooking. The most widely available kind are flat-ish noodles, often labeled "sticks" instead of noodles, that are great in soups (like the Taiwanese-ish soup on page 96) and stir-fried with deeply flavored sauces. They don't require much cooking.

Rice paper wrappers are another member of the dried rice noodle family. Sometimes called spring or summer roll skins, they're used to wrap up delicious things in Southeast Asian cooking. They feel like plastic out of the package, but after a quick soak in hot water, they're ready to use.

6. Wonton/dumpling wrappers

Sure, you could make your own dumpling skins. You could also use simple household tools to take care of your dental health needs. But life is not a big Hey Look What I Can Make competition, so celebrate the little shortcuts, like cheap and plentiful wonton wrappers. The square wrappers lend themselves better to boiling (like in wonton soup) and the round wrappers to pan-frying (think potstickers or gyoza), but the rules here are neither hard nor fast.

7. Somen

Somen are thin wheat noodles from Japan used, most famously, for Hiyashi Somen (page 132), the hot-weather noodle dish.

8. Sweet potato noodles (not pictured)

Like glassy spaghetti with a good chew, these Korean noodles are enjoying a moment because they are recommended on the Paleo diet. (Cavemen loved Korean food.) This means you might be able to find them at your local health food store.

Rice

Almost all of the dishes in this book that don't feature a starch (i.e., noodles or, occasionally, bread) are meant to be eaten with rice. Steamed/boiled/"plain" white rice is the standard accompaniment, but not all white rice is the same. Here's a quick guide:

Chinese, Vietnamese, and most Thai dishes go with jasmine rice. Japanese and Korean dishes go with medium-grain or short-grain ("sushi") rice. Sticky rice is for Thai curries and spicy things—it takes more time than the others, but isn't hard to make. We have eschewed exotic rice varieties in this book, though there's no reason you can't use them.

1. Jasmine

Jasmine rice is a long-grain rice grown (predominantly) in Thailand. It has an extremely subtle floral fragrance, which is where the name comes from.

2. Medium-grain

You can buy a really big bag of medium-grain rice for what you might pay for a regular bag of nice short-grain rice. You might be tempted to see it as the workaday/workhorse Japanese and Korean rice. And maybe it is. It soaks up the stews, sauces, and broths like no other.

3. Sticky (or glutinous)

Sticky rice is the only one you don't cook in a rice cooker. To make it: Bundle up 1½ cups of rice in cheesecloth and submerge it in a bowl of cold water for 3 hours. Then put a steamer over a pot of water that's boiling hard and steam that bundle for 30 minutes. Eat hot or warm. Keep the rice warm and sticky by wrapping the bundle in plastic wrap.

4. Broken

Broken rice is jasmine rice grains that have been, you guessed it, broken during processing. On some level, this is a "lower-quality" rice, but the qualities it has—it sticks together a bit more and strikes me as (unscientifically) more fragrant—are worth a spin every now and again. Included specifically for use with the Vietnamese sausage breakfast on page 68.

5. Short-grain/sushi

The stubby little rice that goes with/in all your Japanese and Korean cooking. There's a real range of this kind of rice that's available, from cheaper, American-grown stuff to fancy Japanese varietals. Our blunt but hopefully helpful Goldilocks advice on that: Don't scrape the bottom of the barrel, but don't reach for the clouds either. The middle is just right.

Pictorial Pantry

Look, we know the Internet is out there. And on it you can find almost anything, from pictures of dogs on surfboards to multilayered analyses of whether or not Thomas Pynchon predicted parallel universes decades before the Hadron Supercollider gave scientists reason to think they might exist. But the pull of *Gravity's Rainbow* aside, what

we wanted to do here was give you a simple visual and factual orientation to what we cooked with as we made this book, so you know what you're looking for as you paw through the aisles of a foreign supermarket and/or the murky depths of third-party seller pages on Amazon.com.

We divided our pantry into basic, intermediate, and champion levels because (a) it would have been really hard to get everything in one shot and (b) these levels reflect the necessity of the ingredients.

Pantry Level 1:
Basic

1. Soy sauce

Our preferred soy sauces are Japanese-made and are labeled *usukuchi,* which is sometimes called "light" soy sauce. (That lightness is in color; do not confuse it with low-sodium soy sauce.) We tested the recipes here with a range of different store brands, and they should work with even the Kikkoman bottle you swiped off the local take-out place's to-go counter.

2. Sesame oil

Don't be afraid to pay a little more for something nicer than basic, but buy a small bottle——a little bit goes a long way, and sesame oil doesn't improve with age.

3. Peanuts

Planter's cocktail peanuts inarguably get the job done and are so widely available you can probably buy them at the gas station.

4. Tahini

Tahini is puréed sesame seeds. Get something from a Middle Eastern grocery if possible.

5. Mirin

Mirin is a sweet, sake-like fermented rice wine product that's a building block of Japanese cuisine. Real mirin is sweet and alcoholic and hard to find outside of a dedicated Japanese grocery; *hon mirin* is what you'll find in most places. It's some sort of debased industrial version of the real deal, sweetened with corn syrup, and it's a 100 percent acceptable substitute that makes perfectly delicious food.

6. Sesame seeds

At *Lucky Peach,* we have one intern whose only job is to harvest sesame seeds off of the top of a few dozen Big Mac buns every week for the test kitchen. If you don't have the means to hire a sesame intern, buy yours in small quantities, as nobody, not even Ronald McDonald, likes rancid old seed.

7. Oyster sauce

A funky sauce made from fermented oysters. Keeps forever.

8. Rice vinegar

Essential. Sometimes called rice wine vinegar. Make sure you're not buying the "seasoned" stuff, which seems to fill the shelves. Rice vinegar is less acidic than white, sherry, and even wine vinegars (at around 4% acidity) so keep that in mind if you're substituting something else for it.

9. Fish sauce

People often invoke the slurping of the first raw oyster when they talk about how crazy it is that we humans eat such a wide range of flora and fauna. For me, I think of the first crazy bastard who stood over a barrel of anchovies covered in rainwater that had been sitting out in the summer sun for weeks and thought to himself, "Oh yeah, I'm gonna sprinkle that juice all over my dinner tonight!"

But he was a genius and I doff my cap to him. Fancy fish sauce—like Red Boat and Megachef—is worth it if you're flush, but if that $6 difference in the price of a bottle bothers you, Squid brand has served me reliably for years.

10. Star anise
The prettiest of all the herbs and spices. When you're shopping for it, look to see that the star-shaped pods are intact.

11. Sambal oelek
A spicy, garlicky chili condiment that is good on everything from pizza to eggs.

12. Miso paste
Funky salty fermented soybeans. Buy a tub of the red (*aka*) miso and a tub of the white (*shiro*) miso. They keep for months in the refrigerator and can be used interchangeably in a pinch.

13. Shaoxing wine
Most of your musty old Asian-ish cookbooks, the forefathers of this book, will note that you can substitute sherry for Shaoxing wine. This is true—they share a similar oxidized flavor. But one day, in the making of this book, we reached beyond the "cooking" Shaoxing wine and ponied up $15 for a beautiful ceramic bottle (pictured with the pickles on page 32) that came in a wooden box (look for it behind the citrus on page 261) and we were blown away by how delicious it was. A little poking around taught us that the Shaoxing wine

that we'd been buying from the condiment aisle is denatured with salt (so that people won't drink it, Thunderbird-style, on the corner) and that the real-deal stuff is not only better, but good enough to sip on at the end of the day. So we'd like to say this: If you're making a Spanish meal and find yourself short on the fino sherry, feel free to substitute premium Shaoxing wine for it. Fancy wine jibber-jabber aside, a $4 bottle of salty Shaoxing will get the job done.

14. Hondashi
Hondashi is instant dashi powder, and looks and smells a lot like fish sauce. While it is not hard at all to make dashi (the method is on page 73), there are some times when hondashi saves the day, and some recipes where using it cuts out an extra couple steps and some mess without compromising quality. It's cheap and keeps forever.

15. Dried shiitakes
Are dried shiitakes. They are called for sparingly in this book, but anytime you're making a broth or stock, you can add one and it will lend it depth and umami. They keep forever, so there's no reason not to have them on hand.

16. Lap cheong (aka Chinese sausage)
When we call for Chinese sausage we are calling for the basic pork variety, though you can substitute others as you like. The kind made "with wine," as some of the packages say, has a nice, buzzy, old-man-with-*baijiu*-breath flavor that I like, and the varieties made with a proportion of liver are sometimes too funky for me. The main thing to know about Chinese sausage is that, like Martin's Potato Rolls or good jam, it should be in your house at all times.

Pantry Level 2:
Intermediate

北海道名産

お徳用

花

かつお

中國特産

五香粉

FIVE SPICE POWDER

OPEN

麻辣脆油辣粉

CHILI CRISP SAUCE

고소하고 감칠맛

북경식 정통짜장

Black Bean Paste
Fermented
Net wt.1.1lbs(500g)

종가비김
태양초
순창 고추장

น้ำพริก MAESRI
RED
CURRY PASTE

น้ำพริกแกงแดง
NET WT. 4 OZ (114g)

MAESRI
GREEN
CURRY PASTE

Nutrition Facts
Amount Per Serving
Calories

Total Carb.

NET WT. 4 OZ (114g)

净含量(113g)
4oz(113g)

1. White pepper

White pepper is the same thing—plant, berry, etc.—as black pepper, just processed in a different manner. The flavor is different—less pungent, spicy, aromatic—and more dusty and mysterious.

2. Sichuan peppercorns

Sichuan peppercorns are not spicy; they are numbing. Essential.

3. Kombu

Kombu is dried kelp, which grows in great forests off of all the most beautiful and rugged coastlines in the world. Any kombu works in the kitchen; the best is from Hokkaido in northern Japan. Simmer or steep (but don't boil) it in a broth to add instant umami.

4. Katsuobushi (bonito flakes)

So you take a bonito fish, you fillet it, you cook the fillets in a crazy umami-rich liquid, you smoke them, then you let them hang and dry until they're as hard as wood. Shave the results, and you've got bonito flakes, an essential Japanese pantry item and kombu's partner in making dashi, the fundamental Japanese stock.

5. Chinkiang vinegar

Chinkiang vinegar is sharp and deep and a little sweet; it's the stuff that shows up in the saucer alongside soup dumplings (*xiao long bao*). It's also called black vinegar, but read the label to make sure it says Chinkiang to know you're getting the right thing (and not the Worcestershire sauce–like product also sold as black vinegar). It should be made with glutinous rice, wheat, salt, sugar, and then whatever magical chemicals the particular manufacturer uses.

6. Chili oil

Chili oil has the *ma la* flavors of Sichuan cuisine—spicy chili heat and numbing peppercorn power—infused into a dangerously innocuous-looking oil. Taste as you go with this stuff, as potency varies from brand to brand.

7. Spicy chili crisp

Do you need this? Not quite. Do you want this? Most definitely. Crisp fried chilies

embedded in oil add a punishing wallop of heat to anything, and the dour-looking lady on the jar is a signifier to other food nerds that you've crossed the sriracha river into the land of freaky-deaky hot sauces that will never be trendy.

8. Nori

Dried seaweed, usually sold in sheets. For the Onigiri (page 150) and most Japanese dishes, you want unseasoned nori. For Korean dishes and feeding to your kids as a snack, you want Korean seasoned nori. Unseasoned nori benefits from being waved over an open flame to wake it up a little bit before it is eaten.

9. Gochujang and gochugaru

So the *gochu* is Korean for chilies, *garu* is flakes, and *jang* is paste. The flavors of Korean dried chilies are distinctive, and *gochujang* has kind of a spicy, seasoned miso paste–type thing going on. If you like Korean food or plan to make any of it, these are essentials.

10. Five-spice powder

Cinnamon and star anise are the flavors that ride out front of most five-spice blends, cloves and fennel seed trailing behind, and peppercorns (sometimes Sichuan) in the rear, never really detectable.

11. Shrimp chips

Get 'em, love 'em, never leave 'em. You will see handsome boxes of shrimp chips in Asian supermarkets, and be tempted to buy them because of their handsome packaging. Do not do this. Buy the already fried chips, two bags at a time, so you can eat one while walking home from the store. (Okay, okay, it's not hard at all to fry up the boxed chips; all you need is hot oil. But bagged chips are inarguably easier and just as good.)

12. Curry paste

Curry powder is a by-product of British colonialism that has no real basis in Indian cuisine. Canned or jarred Southeast Asian curry pastes are entirely different; they are food technology doing a good thing, by putting deliciousness within shelf-stable reach. It's worth having a jar or can of red and green varieties of this stuff in the cupboard at all times because it's packed with flavor and easy to use.

Pantry Level 3:

Champion

1. Dried baby shrimp

Dried shrimp can be bought in little packages from Asian supermarkets or loose, by weight, in the kinds of Chinatown stores that sell dried things and ginseng. We call for them twice in this book, as a flavoring for the dipping sauce in Hiyashi Somen (page 132) and pounded into the dressing of the Green Papaya Salad (page 56).

2. Takuan

A giant yellow daikon radish pickle that's a popular kimbap ingredient, and a common companion to all manner of Japanese and Korean meals. It's sweet, slightly sour, and strangely addictive. We use takuan in Spicy Mushroom Ragu (page 137), though you could swap in canned Sichuan pickled radish for it there if you can find the Chinese one.

3. Dried lotus leaves

Like corn husks, these are inedible and lend a distinctive and inimitable aroma to foods

wrapped and steamed in them. They're also gigantic, hard to store, and hard to find, so we understand if you make the *lap mei fan* (Sticky Rice Wrapped in Lotus Leaves, page 155) without them.

4. Dried red chilies

You can use what I call "pizza flakes" for 100 percent of the dried spicy needs in this book and everything will come out delicious. But thin-skinned Chinese dried chilies do have their own charms and are worth keeping a quart of around, for spicing up your Kung Pao Shrimp (page 238) or your Braised Chicken Wings (page 198).

5. Dried wood ear mushrooms

Meaty, umami-rich dried mushrooms that, if the pictures on the box I bought them in are right, grow on the sides of trees in some unspoiled misty mountain corner of China. They are of limited use, sure, but it's a low cost and big return on investment.

Use them and your Hot and Sour Soup (page 110) achieves greatness.

6. Maltose

Maltose is a kind of sugar. You need to warm it up to work with it, and it's sticky like superglue the whole time. But it adds a funky, toasty sweetness that has a familiar Chinatown flavor to it, and it has the ability to brown foods to a comic book color, like the Lacquered Roast Chicken on page 183. Not essential and somewhat of a pain in the ass to handle, but recommended for the intrepid. Honey is a reasonable substitution.

7. Furikake

Furikake is a Japanese condiment that is a blend of dried seaweed and different seasonings—sesame seeds, dehydrated fish, puffed rice, the sky seems to be the limit. We recommend keeping a jar in the house at all times because rice + a runny egg + furikake = delicious dinner. The equation works even without an egg.

8. Shichimi togarashi

A Japanese hot pepper–black pepper mix. More for seasoning finished dishes than using in cooking; delicious.

9. Umeboshi

Intensely flavored pickled tiny plums from Japan. A little bit goes a long way.

10. Preserved black beans

Real talk: Preserved black beans stink like a dead animal left out on hot asphalt. Another truth: They add an incredibly delicious umami note when added in even tiny amounts to a dish. Keep them in a tightly sealed container in a cabinet you don't open that often, but keep them. And explore their savory wonderfulness in recipes like the Black Bean Sauce (page 242) for a steamed whole fish. Rinse before using.

Cold Dishes, Apps, and Pickly Bits

Soy 'n' Sugar Cucumber Pickles

Makes 1 pint

12 oz	Persian or Japanese cucumber, cut into ¼" rounds
⅓ C	soy sauce
3 T	brown sugar
3 T	rice vinegar
¼ t	fennel seeds

1 Combine the ingredients in a small saucepan. Bring to a boil over medium-high heat and cook for 1 minute, stirring a couple of times to make sure the cucumbers are coated.

2 Transfer the cucumbers and pickling liquid to a pint jar. The cucumbers should be completely submerged. Let cool, then cover and chill for at least 12 hours. Pickles will keep, covered and refrigerated, for up to 2 weeks.

We picked these sweet and savory pickles out of Chris Ying's mom's meatloaf recipe. They're the Chinese answer to bread 'n' butter pickles, and great as a side dish, with drinks, or anyplace you'd stick a little brown pickle, like Lamburgers (page 210).

Chineasy Cucumber Salad

Makes about 2 servings, easily multiplied

1 T	Chinkiang vinegar
1 t	Sichuan chili oil
1 t	sesame oil
1 t	turbinado sugar
¼ t	kosher salt
3	Persian or Kirby cucumbers or 1 English cucumber
1 t	toasted sesame seeds
2 T	crushed roasted unsalted peanuts
2 T	cilantro leaves

1 Whisk together the vinegar, chili oil, sesame oil, sugar, and salt in a medium bowl until the sugar dissolves. Set the dressing aside.

2 Halve the cucumbers lengthwise. (If using English cucumbers, remove the seeds with a small spoon and discard.) Set them cut-side down on a cutting board and lightly smash them: Give them a couple angry thwaps with the side of a cleaver (or a large chef's knife) until the cucumbers crack in a few places. (For less drama, just press down on them with the side of the knife.) Cut the abused cucumbers crosswise into ¾-inch-thick half-moons.

3 Toss the cucumbers in the dressing, portion them out onto plates, and top each serving with sesame seeds, peanuts, and cilantro.

Cucumbers are best in the summer, but hothouse specimens are in the supermarket and in most of our refrigerators year-round. This is a treatment that will perk up even the most chemically enhanced wintertime cuke.

This salad takes cues from Xi'an cooking (specifically the kind channeled at restaurants like Xi'an Famous Foods and Mission Chinese Food), pinning down the cooling flavor of cucumber under a savory-sour blast of black vinegar and a sting of chili heat. Do not skip the peanuts; like the rug in *The Big Lebowski,* they really tie the room together. And feel free to amp up the cilantro if you're so inclined.

Silken Tofu Snack

Makes 1 or 2 servings

8 oz	block silken tofu
½	avocado
2 T	soy sauce
1 t	lime juice
½ t	olive oil
1 T	furikake

Cut the tofu into ½-inch-thick slices and arrange them on a plate. Scoop the avocado out of the skin and thinly slice. Shingle the avocado across the top of the tofu. Drizzle with the soy sauce, lime juice, and olive oil, then sprinkle with the furikake. Eat immediately.

The image we have created here, of champagne and golden chopsticks, stands in direct contrast to the genesis of this dish: Chris Ying, illustrious editor in chief of *Lucky Peach*, arrives home from a late-night soccer scrimmage. He is sweaty and starving, and while his truest self wants to assemble a self-hate burrito from the leftovers in the corners of his fridge, the high-achiever inside tells him, *Build on the healthy thing you just did*. He mixes tofu with avocado, he seasons it with everything in sight, he eats it leaning over the sink. He is sated, at least for the moment.

If you wanna give yourself the champagne-room treatment, seek out *shiro shoyu*, a fancy and hard-to-find "white" soy sauce from Japan that is Ying's preferred condiment here.

Oshitashi

8 oz	greens (such as spinach, Swiss chard, kale, or mustard greens), stemmed and cut into 2" pieces
+	kosher salt
½ t	hondashi dissolved in ½ C hot water (or ½ C Dashi, page 73)
½ t	mirin
1½ t	soy sauce
2 t	toasted sesame seeds, for garnish

1 Blanch the greens in a large pot of boiling, lightly salted water until wilted, about 1 minute. Drain and set aside in a strainer or colander. When cool enough to handle, squeeze the greens dry.

2 Meanwhile, whisk together the hondashi, mirin, and soy sauce in a large bowl.

3 Fold in the greens. Cover and chill for at least 1 hour and up to 24 hours.

4 Reserving the marinade, use clean hands to squeeze the marinade out of the greens—they don't need to be dry, but they shouldn't be drippy-wet either. Pile the greens in little bowls, drizzle with a small spoonful of the reserved marinade, and sprinkle with the sesame seeds. Serve chilled.

Leafy greens (traditionally spinach but feel free to cut loose with whatever greens you like) are given a subtly smoky, umami underpinning from a soak in dashi and soy. Oshitashi is served cold and refreshing in little piles, suitable for shared grazing or individual hoarding. It is a great make-ahead way to add greens to a meal without a bunch of à la minute work.

Seaweed Salad

Makes 4 servings

1 oz	dried wakame
2 T	rice vinegar
1 T	sesame oil
1 T	sugar
1 T	soy sauce
1 t	grated fresh ginger
2 T	toasted sesame seeds
2 T	minced scallion
1	small dried red chili, crumbled, or ½ t chili flakes (optional)

1 Rehydrate the wakame by soaking it in a bowlful of cold water for 5 minutes, or until tender. Drain the seaweed and pat dry with paper towels. Slice any large pieces into ¼-inch strips.

2 Whisk together the vinegar, sesame oil, sugar, soy sauce, and ginger in a medium bowl. Add the seaweed, sesame seeds, scallion, and chili (if using), and toss to coat. Refrigerate until ready to serve.

Perhaps you are among the enlightened sophisticates who already count kelp as a dietary staple. If so, you know this dish. If you're not already a seaweeder, at some point in the not terribly distant future, when we've burnt holes in the sky and there's no snow left on the mountaintops, those of us who didn't get rich in the fast-casual restaurant business before the collapse will be getting our protein from bugs or seaweed. I'd rather be in the latter camp, and this is one way to make seaweed taste good.

Apocalyptic ramblings aside, this is a solid side dish to all manner of Japanese, Korean, and/or misguidedly healthy home-cooked meals you might make. See you in Bartertown.

Soy Sauce Kimchi

Makes 1 quart

1 lb	napa cabbage, cut into 1" pieces
½	Asian pear or 1 medium apple (about 6 oz), grated
½ C	chopped scallions
1½ T	julienned fresh ginger
1	garlic clove, grated
1½ t	gochugaru or other chili flakes
1 T	sugar
+	pinch of kosher salt
½ C	soy sauce
½ C	water

1 Toss together the cabbage, Asian pear, scallions, ginger, garlic, and chili flakes in a large bowl. Sprinkle the sugar and salt over the mixture and massage it. You want the cabbage to wilt under your loving touch until it occupies about half the volume it did when you started. Add the soy sauce and water.

2 Transfer the kimchi and all of its liquid to a gallon zip-top bag, pressing to remove all air. Chill for at least 1 hour for the flavors to meld and develop. Kimchi can be prepared 3 days in advance and refrigerated until ready to serve.

You know how it's really, like, cool to ferment things these days? And how you want to be cool too, but you don't actually ever do enough planning in advance to ferment things for when you need them, or if you do get it together you end up leaving most of the jar of [insert hip fermented product] in the back of the fridge until the very sight of it fills you with shame and you begin to dread it like an envelope of white powder in the Pentagon mailroom?

Well then, soy sauce kimchi is the solution for you! It's basically a make-ahead salad with kimchi flavors, not the deeply fermented funk that scars Korean-American children's memories of opening their lunch boxes in grade school. A kimchi like this is traditionally served as a salad or side dish, though you could also give it the nouveau Korean treatment and stick it in a quesadilla or on top of a hot dog.

Summer Rolls

Makes 12 rolls

3 oz	bean thread/cellophane/rice vermicelli noodles
1 C	shredded napa cabbage
½ C	shredded carrot
½ C	peeled, seeded, and shredded (or julienned) cucumber
¼ C	picked mint leaves
¼ C	picked and torn basil leaves
¼ C	picked cilantro sprigs
¼ C	chopped scallions
+	kosher salt
1–2 t	rice vinegar
12	rice paper wrappers (8½")
18	cooked medium shrimp, peeled and halved lengthwise
+	hoisin sauce and **Nuoc Cham** (page 252), for serving

1 Soak the noodles in hot water to cover in a heatproof bowl until they're softened, about 15 minutes. Drain and transfer to a medium bowl.

2 Add the cabbage, carrot, cucumber, mint, basil, cilantro, and scallions to the noodles and toss together. Season lightly with salt and the vinegar. Set the noodle salad aside.

3 Fill a large bowl or pie plate with warm water. Slide a rice paper wrapper into the water and press with your fingertips to submerge it. Lift the wrapper out with both hands, flip it, and place it back into the water. Continue flipping and soaking until the wrapper is soft and pliable, about 30 seconds, then lay it flat on a kitchen towel or several layers of paper towels.

4 Working with one at a time, lay a rice paper wrapper on your work surface. Arrange 3 shrimp halves in a row near one edge of the wrapper. Top with about ⅓ cup (a three-finger pinch) of the noodle salad, then roll the nearest edge of the wrapper over the filling. Fold in the sides of the wrapper and continue to roll up to seal. Transfer, shrimp-side up, to a platter. Repeat with the remaining wrappers, shrimp, and noodle salad until you have 12 rolls. Chill, draped with a damp paper towel, for up to 1 hour.

5 Halve the rolls crosswise at an angle; serve with nuoc cham and hoisin sauces for dipping.

Ninety percent of the work required to make these summer rolls is in the shopping; the remainder is in feigning exhaustion at having produced such spectacular snacks for your friends. In between, all you need to do is toss vegetables, herbs, and noodles in a light seasoning, then roll that salad up with some sliced shrimp into cute little rice-paper burritos!

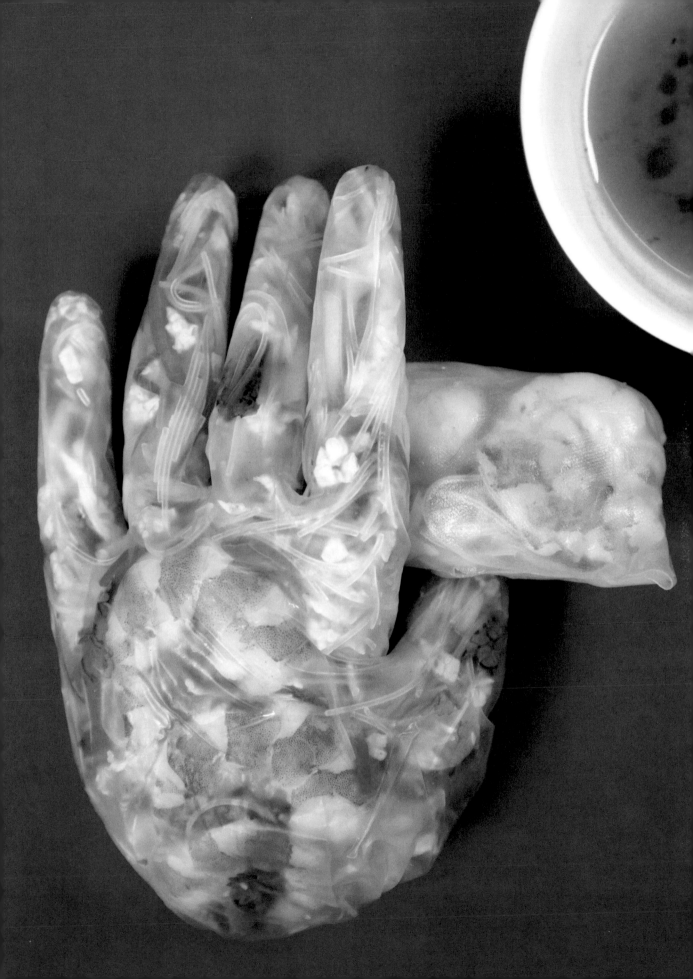

Gado Gado Dip

Makes about 1 cup (enough for 4 servings)

1	fresh red chili, such as Holland or Fresno, or ¼–½ t chili flakes
1	garlic clove
½ C	peanut butter
3 T	lime juice
3 T	brown sugar
2 T	fish sauce
1 T	soy sauce
¼ C	hot water
+	kosher salt

Combine the chili, garlic, peanut butter, lime juice, sugar, fish sauce, and soy sauce in a blender and process until smooth. With the blender running, drizzle in the hot water and process until creamy. It should have a honey-like consistency. If it doesn't, add more water by the tablespoon. Season to taste with salt. The dip will keep, covered and refrigerated, for 3 days.

What is authenticity? Who knows! But a dip is easy to recognize. This one is a compulsively eatable way to make a dinner out of vegetables and a compelling argument for the compatibility of peanut butter and broccoli.

Shrimp chips:
Don't front. You gotta have shrimp chips. And don't be a hero and try to fry them yourself—just buy a couple bags.

Firm tofu:
Cut the tofu into two-bit pieces and serve chilled or blanched for 30 seconds in boiling, lightly salted water.

Carrots:
Cut into coins or sticks and blanch in boiling salted water until nearly tender, about 3 minutes. Shock in ice water, drain, and pat dry.

Broccoli or cauliflower:
Cut a head into bite-size florets. Blanch briefly in boiling salted water, just until the stalks yield to the tip of a paring knife, about 2 minutes. Shock in ice water and drain on a plate lined with paper towels.

Green beans/long beans:
Trim and blanch the beans in a pot of boiling salted water until bright green and still snappy, barely a minute. Shock in ice water, drain, and pat dry.

Boiled eggs:
You don't know how to boil eggs? Fine: Put the eggs in a snug single layer in a saucepan, cover by 1 inch with cold water, and set the pan over high heat. Once the water boils, remove from the heat and let stand 8 minutes. Drain and shock in ice water, then crack and peel the eggs. Slice or cut into wedges before serving.

Cabbage:
Arrange 1-inch-wide wedges of cabbage in a baking dish, sprinkle with salt, cover with a kettleful of boiling water, and soak until translucent. Remove with tongs, keeping the wedges intact, and drain on paper towels.

Scallion Salad

Makes 4 side-dish or garnish servings

1	bunch scallions (about ½ lb)
1 T	rice vinegar
1 T	sugar
2 t	sesame oil
1 t	gochugaru or other chili flakes

1 Set up a bowl of ice and water. Cut the scallions crosswise into 3-inch pieces, then slice lengthwise into thin matchsticks. Place in the bowl of ice water and soak for at least 20 minutes—the scallions will curl, crisp, and mellow. (If not serving immediately, refrigerate until ready to use, up to 12 hours.)

2 When ready to serve, whisk together the vinegar, sugar, sesame oil, and chili flakes until the sugar dissolves.

3 Drain the scallions and pat dry with paper towels. Toss with the dressing and serve.

Scallion salad is one of the thousand things you might see served as *banchan*, that procession of little dishes that accompanies Korean meals. It's great with all grilled meats and fishes, and would be a good ride-along to any of the Korean dishes in this book. But you could just as easily decide you want to put it on hot dogs or hamburgers—who's stopping you, right?

One helpful note if you don't want to get carpal tunnel syndrome while finely julienning all those scallions: Korean and Japanese markets sell something called a scallion-cutter, a sharp little razor rake that makes slicing up the scallions waaaaay less of a chore. And bigger Korean grocery stores will sell bags of already-sliced scallions that you can bring home, freshen up in some ice water, and dress to taste.

Soy Sauce Eggs

Makes 6 eggs

3 T	soy sauce
2 T	rice vinegar
1 T	brown sugar
1 T	water
¼ t	chili flakes (optional)
1	point star anise (optional)
¼ t	black peppercorns (optional)
6	large hard-boiled eggs, peeled

Combine the soy sauce, vinegar, sugar, water, and spices (if using) in a small saucepan. Bring the sauce to a simmer over medium heat. Add as many of the eggs as will fit with some room to roll around. Gently swirl the pan, rolling the eggs in the sauce. Continue rolling around until the eggs are tan and infused with the soy, about 5 minutes. Using a slotted spoon, remove the eggs and transfer to a plate to cool. Repeat with any remaining eggs. Let the eggs cool, then refrigerate for up to 2 days (after which they'll be safe but getting too salty).

Make deviled eggs with them! Top your ramen with them! Eat them straight out of the fridge or in the driver's seat of your big rig on an overnight long haul! Honk!

Spicy Cold Celery

Makes 4 servings

1 T	soy sauce
1 T	sesame oil
1 T	rice vinegar
1 t	sugar
1 t	spicy chili crisp or chili oil (or 1 t sambal oelek plus a few crushed Sichuan peppercorns)
4	large celery stalks, sliced thinly on an angle (about 2½ C)

Stir together the soy sauce, sesame oil, vinegar, sugar, and chili crisp in a medium bowl until the sugar dissolves. Add the celery and fold to coat it in the dressing. Let stand 5 minutes and then eat. The celery will keep in the fridge, getting spicier all the while, for about 3 days.

I love this recipe, firstly because it gives me something to do with celery, which is always available and almost always languishing in the crisper of my refrigerator. Secondly, because it's a great place to use a jarred sauce called "spicy chili crisp," which you, like me, may be tempted to buy when you're wandering the hot sauce aisle of your Chinese supermarket. The sauce is irresistible on account of its dragon's-breath heat, the pleasing way the texture of the crisp fried chilies makes all foods more exciting to eat, and because of the reproachful look of the woman on the label. (Don't worry about that sourpuss getting an unfair shake in life: Her name is Tao Huabi and she created the sauce and the company, Lao Gan Ma, that sells it. Her net worth is in the hundreds of millions!) Seek it out if you like hot options in the fridge, or use one of the recommended substitutes above.

Dashimaki Tamago

Makes 1 omelet (1 or 2 servings)

3	large eggs
½ t	sugar
½ t	hondashi dissolved in ½ C hot water (or use **Dashi,** page 73)
+	vegetable oil spray
+	grated daikon, for serving
+	soy sauce, for serving

1 Whisk together the eggs, sugar, and 6 tablespoons of the hondashi liquid in a measuring cup with a spout. There will be about 1 cup.

2 Heat an 8- to 10-inch nonstick skillet over medium-low heat and spray with oil. Pour in just enough egg mixture to coat the bottom of the pan, about ¼ cup. When the egg is starting to set, use a silicone spatula or a pair of chopsticks to fold it over on itself, starting at the side away from the handle with a fold of about ½ inch. Continue folding/rolling the omelet until you reach the handle. Push the omelet back to the far side of the skillet, away from the handle.

3 Pour more egg mixture in, again just enough to cover the bottom. Lift the already rolled omelet to allow some of the uncooked egg mixture to run underneath. Repeat the rolling procedure, beginning with the far end, so you're rolling the second omelet around the first. Keep the heat low enough so that the egg is not becoming dry and brown, but rather staying tender and lightly golden. Repeat this step until you've used up all of the egg mixture.

4 You can serve the omelet right away at this point, but a common (and easy) refinement/way to shape the omelet is to set the omelet on a clean, dry kitchen towel (or a sushi mat if you live that lifestyle) and roll it into a rectangular tube, pressing gently to shape the omelet. Let stand several minutes before unwrapping and slicing crosswise into 1-inch pieces. Serve with grated daikon and soy sauce for drizzling.

Dashi is a fundamental ingredient in Japanese cooking. Here it makes eggs lighter and better. I always thought making this kind of omelet was some next-level ninja thing until we started work on this book. Now I know it can be made in 10 minutes flat, and the worst thing that will happen is that it won't be as pretty as the one in the picture. With a salad or vegetable and a bowl of rice, it's dinner!

Green Papaya Salad

1 T	dried baby shrimp
1	garlic clove, minced
¼ C	palm or brown sugar
2 t	sambal oelek
1 C	pieces (2") green beans
¼ C	lime juice
¼ C	fish sauce
1 C	cherry tomatoes, halved
4 C	shredded green papaya (from ½ medium green papaya weighing about 2½ lb)
¼ C	roasted unsalted peanuts

1 Combine the shrimp, garlic, sugar, and sambal in a large mortar and pound into a paste with the pestle. Add the beans and pound gently to bruise them. Add the lime juice, fish sauce, and tomatoes and stir with a spoon, lightly crushing the tomatoes to release their juices.

2 Scoop the vegetable mixture into a large bowl. Add the papaya and peanuts and toss to combine.

We tried to skimp as hard as we could on the specialty equipment needed to make the recipes in this book, but classic Pepsi-vs.-Coke-style blind taste tests proved that the mortar makes the magic when it comes to this classic Thai salad. You could use a food processor, but there's just something about the not-quite-uniformity of pounding with a pestle (rather than hacking with blades) that improves the seasoning paste. Plus you can't really bruise green beans with a food processor.

If you're shopping in a Thai market, you'll probably see papaya shredders for sale and think they're good for this. After numerous tests, our conclusion is this: They are okay. The cheap and cheerful Japanese and Chinese mandoline you may already have in your kitchen gadget drawer is less authentic and more effective. Use that to shred the fruit.

Try Making
Dumplings

When the staff of *Lucky Peach* convened for the ideation session that birthed this book, there was much to sort out: First, how to thank Richard Branson for giving us free reign over his fully staffed and privately owned island for the better part of a month, and, later, whether or not dumplings are easy. The physical act of making them is, inarguably, easy. There is no great challenge in folding them closed, and even if your first dumpling is fugly, the fortieth will be respectable looking, and by your hundredth you'll be muttering under your breath in Chinese, wondering when the mah-jongg game is gonna get started. Ultimately we decided—and this was after tiring out scores of Mr. Branson's masseuses and drinking most of his pre-*Botrytis* champagne—that they were worthy of inclusion because the return on the investment of effort was high. Dumplings are good to eat, fun to eat, and you'll usually make more than you can eat in one go of it—so you're laying down supplies for the future, for a day when you don't have the time to stuff them. Once the motion was ratified, we went skinny-dipping in the lagoon, but that's a story for a different time.

Dollar Dumplings

Makes 8 servings

1 lb	ground pork
¼ C	minced scallions
1 T	minced fresh ginger
1 T	soy sauce
1 T	Shaoxing wine
1 t	cornstarch
1 t	sugar
½ t	sesame oil
+	white pepper
40	round dumpling wrappers
+	neutral oil
+	**Dumpling Dipping Sauce** (opposite), for serving

1 Mix together the pork, scallions, ginger, soy sauce, wine, cornstarch, sugar, sesame oil, and a few turns of white pepper in a bowl. (A hand, gloved or otherwise, probably does the best job of kneading it all together.)

2 Fill each dumpling wrapper with a scant tablespoon of filling. Moisten the edges of the wrapper with water and pleat them shut, following the drawings on page 62. You can cook the dumplings right away or arrange them in a single layer on a baking sheet (keeping everything dusted with extra cornstarch to prevent sticking), wrap well in plastic, and refrigerate for a day or two. Or do the thing with the baking sheet/cornstarch/plastic wrap and FREEZE the dumplings, then transfer them, once frozen, to zip-top bags for easier storage and access.

3 Cook the dumplings in one of two ways:

Pan-fried: A 12-inch cast iron skillet is the ideal vessel for this; any similarly brawny large skillet will do. Add enough neutral oil to generously coat the bottom of the pan, then a little bit more. Place the pan over medium heat and add the dumplings to the pan, arranging them pleats-up in a neatly nestled layer that covers the entirety of the pan. (You will need to cook two or three batches of dumplings from a recipe this size.)

Once the oil is good and sizzling, count 30 seconds off, then pour ¼ cup-ish of water into the skillet and cover with a lid. That water will turn into steam, which is what is really cooking your dumplings. After 3 minutes, remove the lid and poke a dumpling: The filling should be firm like a meatball and the wrapper tender like properly cooked pasta. If the pans dries out before the dumplings are cooked, add another little splash of water and cover again. When they are cooked, uncover and let the water boil off and the dumplings thoroughly crisp and brown on the bottoms. They will release from the pan when they are done. Transfer to a serving tray or Styrofoam clamshells for to-go orders. Repeat for the remaining dumplings.

Boiled: Put a large pot of water on to boil. Boil the dumplings in batches that don't crowd the pot—10 to 12 maximum at a time. They should be ready in 3 to 4 minutes, when the filling is firm to the touch. Remove with a slotted spoon or spider to a serving platter.

Dollar Dumplings II: Replace all the aromatics in this recipe (the scallions through the white pepper) with 3 tablespoons of either of the ginger-scallion sauces (page 246).

Dollar Dumplings III: Cabbage-ify your dumplings for extra juiciness: Add 1 cup (8 ounces) salted and squeezed cabbage (see step 1 of Vegetable Dumplings, page 64) to the pork filling.

Dumpling Dipping Sauce

Makes ⅓ cup

3 T	soy sauce
1 T	rice vinegar
1 t	sugar
2 T	water
+	couple drops of sesame oil

Stir together the ingredients in a small bowl. Serve with dumplings.

Sauceless dumplings are like the crying-on-the-inside kind of clowns: They look the part but something important is missing.

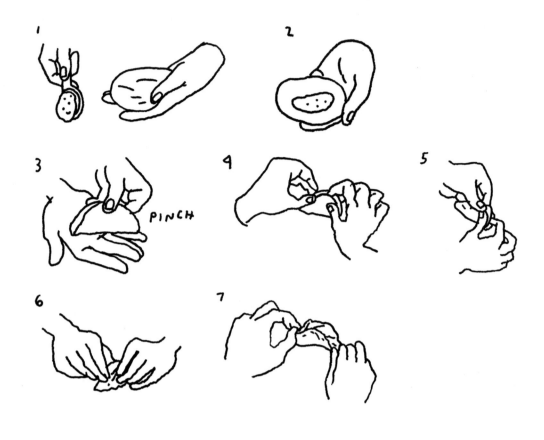

One of the most important things to keep in mind when you're stuffing dumplings is that more is not always more: Trying to stuff too much in the wrappers leads to unruly, overly plump, portly dumplings that comport themselves poorly, spitting out filling on one side or the other as you try to crimp them shut, or bursting in an unseemly fashion in the pan. A teaspoon of filling is ample.

Then there's the folding of them: What we have illustrated above (and also shown in the opening photo on page 59) is a pleated style, like you find in dollar dumpling shops in Chinatown and/or in the freezer case at Trader Joe's. After placing a prim teaspoon of filling in the center of the wrapper, you moisten first your finger and then the wrapper's rim with water, then lightly pinch it shut. Then, working from one side to the other, you make tiny pleats, like you are the Issey Miyake of hot appetizers. Superchef Martin Yan once narrated this action to us, rhythmically chanting: PUSH, PLEAT, PUSH, PLEAT. And while it sounds more like a dance-floor anthem then a cooking instruction, with a dumpling in your hands it will make sense.

Also, look at the photo on page 65, where, lurking in broth in the back of the shot, we have our shrimp dumplings folding in a very #basic wonton-soup style. To effect that look, place a teaspoon of dumpling in the middle of the wrapper, moisten it, fold it shut (into a half-moon), and then fold the edges into the middle, affixing them with water. This is a go-to folding style for dumplings that are going to be served in soup or broth, and for when square wrappers are all you can find.

Shrimp and Chive Dumplings

Makes 8 servings

1 lb	shelled shrimp, minced
1 C	very finely chopped chives (if you can find garlic chives, so much the better)
1 T	minced fresh ginger
1	egg, lightly beaten
1 T	soy sauce
1 T	Shaoxing wine
½ t	sesame oil
½ t	white pepper
½ t	kosher salt
40	square wonton skins
+	cornstarch
+	**Dumpling Dipping Sauce** (page 61), for serving

1 Stir together the shrimp, chives, ginger, egg, soy sauce, wine, sesame oil, white pepper, and salt in a large bowl.

2 Stuff and store the dumplings as directed in Dollar Dumplings (page 60).

3 Put a large pot of water on to boil. Boil the dumplings in batches that don't crowd the pot—10 to 12 maximum at a time. They should be ready in 3 to 4 minutes, when the filling is firm to the touch. Remove with a slotted spoon or spider to a serving platter. Alternatively, we like these dumplings in a bath of simple chicken broth or, if you're getting really fancy, as an addition to the Chicken Noodle Soup (page 102).

Vegetable Dumplings

Makes 8 servings

1 lb	napa cabbage (1 small head or ½ large)
1 t	kosher salt
+	neutral oil
8 oz	fresh shiitake mushroom caps, thinly sliced
1 T	minced fresh ginger
1 T	minced garlic
1 T	soy sauce
2 t	cornstarch
40	round dumpling wrappers
+	**Dumpling Dipping Sauce** (page 61), for serving

1 Cut the cabbage lengthwise into 3 or 4 long pieces, then thinly slice crosswise to create matchstick-size pieces. Put the cabbage in a bowl and sprinkle with ½ teaspoon of the salt. Massage the salt into the cabbage and let stand until it is wilted and weeping some juice, about 10 minutes. Squeeze the cabbage firmly to release as much liquid as possible. The squeezed cabbage should weigh about 8 ounces, and there will be about 1 heaping cup of it.

2 Heat about 1 tablespoon oil in a large skillet over medium-low heat. Add the mushrooms and sprinkle with the remaining ½ teaspoon salt. Cook, stirring frequently, until the mushrooms' liquid is drawn out and then evaporates, about 8 minutes.

3 Once the mushrooms are tender and the pan is dry, fold in the cabbage. Cook until the mixture is again dry, but not cooked to death, a couple of minutes. Scrape the mixture into a bowl and let cool slightly.

4 Add the ginger, garlic, soy sauce, and cornstarch to the mushroom-cabbage mixture and stir to combine. Taste for seasoning.

5 Stuff, store, and cook the dumplings as directed in Dollar Dumplings (page 60).

Breakfast

Com Tam Breakfast

Makes 4 servings

Sausage

1 lb	ground pork
½ C	minced shallot
3 T	minced garlic
3 T	minced lemongrass
1 T	sugar
1 T	fish sauce
½ t	freshly ground black pepper
+	kosher salt
+	oil

Assembly

+	steamed broken rice or jasmine rice
+	fried eggs
+	**Nuoc Cham** (page 252), for dousing
+	cilantro, mint, and basil

1 Make the sausage: Using your hands, knead together the pork, shallot, garlic, lemongrass, sugar, fish sauce, and pepper in a large bowl. Pick up and slap the mixture back into the bowl several times until the meat feels slightly tacky, like the shaggy stage of bread dough. (The sausage can also be beaten for 30 seconds on low speed in a stand mixer outfitted with the paddle attachment.) Cook a tablespoon of the meat in a small skillet and taste for seasoning; add a sprinkle of salt to the sausage mix if needed. Cover and chill for at least 30 minutes and up to 24 hours.

2 Form the sausage into 2-inch patties with oiled hands. Heat a slick of oil in a heavy skillet over medium heat and fry the patties, flipping once, until they are swollen in the middle and browned. Let rest for a couple of minutes before serving.

3 Serve with rice, eggs, nuoc cham, and herbs.

Com tam is broken rice, an ingredient, but also the name of a family of dishes that could generally be described as "broken rice with stuff on top of them." In a particularly thrifty case, that stuff might be just some pickled or lightly sauced vegetables. Often there's pork, and eggs are common. Our com tam is a mash-up of a lemongrass-y pork sausage that chef Tien Ho served at Momofuku Ssäm Bar + a version of a dish that Danny Bowien serves for Vietnamese breakfast at his Mexican restaurant, Mission Cantina.

A couple notes: Don't let not having any one element keep you from making this dish—even the titular com tam could be swapped out for jasmine rice. In fact you could scrap the whole setup and just use this sausage like it's some kinda Vietnamese Jimmy Dean action in a sausage and egg sandwich and probably still be happy.

St. Paul Sandwich

Makes 2 sandwiches

Egg Foo Yung

3 T	neutral oil
1 C	bean sprouts
½ C	thinly sliced scallions
2 T	minced serrano or green bell pepper
1 t	soy sauce
+	kosher salt
+	white pepper
¼ C	diced cooked ham, chicken, or beef (optional)
2	large eggs
1 T	cornstarch

Assembly

4	slices white sandwich bread, lightly toasted
2 T	mayonnaise
5–6	iceberg lettuce leaves
1	tomato, sliced
8	dill pickle chips

1 Make the egg foo yung: Heat 1 tablespoon oil in a large heavy skillet over medium heat. Add the bean sprouts, scallions, and serrano and cook, stirring, until the vegetables are sizzling and slightly wilted, about 3 minutes. Transfer to a bowl and let cool slightly. Season the mixture with the soy sauce and a few pinches of salt and white pepper. Stir in the meat (if using).

2 Crack the eggs into a bowl, then add the cornstarch and beat with a fork to combine. Pour over the vegetable mixture and stir until everything is coated with egg.

3 Reheat the skillet over medium-low heat and slick with 1 tablespoon oil. Scoop half of the egg batter into the pan and use a spatula to coax it into a tight 4-inch-wide fritter/pancake/patty. Cook until the edges are brown and set, then flip, and continue cooking until the patty is slightly puffed and cooked through, about 6 minutes total. Transfer to a plate lined with paper towels to drain. Repeat to make 2 pancakes. Keep warm.

4 Assemble the sandwiches: Spread the toasted bread with mayonnaise and top with lettuce, tomato, pickles, and an egg foo yung pancake.

The story of this sandwich goes something like this: Chinese immigrants build railroads across the continent. Egg foo yung—which is not quite a Chinese dish but has become this iconically Chinese dish to Americans—travels with them as they settle. Somebody in St. Louis, Missouri, liberates an egg foo yung pancake from the brown sauce hell it was doomed to (EFY traditionally being these little egg pancakes ensconced in cornstarchy brown sauce like saber-toothed tigers in a tar pit) and sticks it in the sort of sandwich setup more often reserved for fried chicken cutlets or sliced ham. The results are inarguably good, and somehow get attributed to someone from St. Paul, Minnesota, where the sandwich is entirely foreign.

Weird story, good sandwich!

Miso Soup

Makes 4 servings

¼ C	red miso
1 T	hondashi dissolved in 4 C simmering water (or use **Dashi,** opposite)
2	shiitake mushroom caps, thinly sliced
3 oz	silken tofu, cubed
2 T	chopped scallions

1 Whisk the miso with 2 tablespoons of the hondashi liquid until it dissolves. Pour the remaining hondashi liquid into a medium saucepan and warm to a bare simmer over medium heat. Stir the dissolved miso into the dashi.

2 Add the mushrooms, tofu, and scallions to the broth and gently simmer until everything is warm, about 3 minutes.

A neglected gym membership, unpaid taxes, the parched houseplants on the windowsills: Life's obvious small failures surround us. But what about the failures we might fail to notice? The Rumsfeldian unknown unknowns of living life to its fullest potential? I would argue that not making miso soup is one of those daily missteps that can befall even the most present-minded and successful among us.

Fortunately this is an easy error to correct, easier than washboarding your abs or greening your thumbs. In Japan, miso soup is a beverage almost as much as it is a foodstuff. It is a breakfast thing, served with rice and pickles (and, if you stay at a really fancy hotel, about twenty other delicious dishes, from simmered tofu to grilled fish!). It's a fun thing to work into your morning rotation, especially if you've got a rice cooker that can be programmed to have fresh rice cooked and ready when you wake up.

Dashi

Makes 4 cups

4 C	water
1 or 2	sheets kombu
1	large handful bonito flakes

Bring the water to a simmer in a small pan, add the kombu, and turn the heat off. Let steep for 5 to 10 minutes. (Longer won't hurt, either.) Remove the kombu and discard, then bring back to a simmer. Add the bonito flakes, turn the heat off, and steep for 2 to 3 minutes. Strain and use as needed.

Nasi Lemak

Makes 4 servings

Coconut Rice

2 C	jasmine rice, rinsed and drained
1½ C	water
1	small can (about 5 oz) coconut milk or ½ C plus 2 T
1	bay leaf
+	kosher salt

Sambal Ikan Bilis

1 T	neutral oil
½ C	dried anchovies
½ C	sliced shallot or red onion
¼ C	sambal oelek
1 T	turbinado sugar
1–2 T	lime juice
+	kosher salt

Assembly

3	hard-boiled eggs, peeled and quartered
2	cucumbers, sliced on an angle
+	cocktail peanuts

1 Make the coconut rice: Combine the rice, water, coconut milk, bay leaf, and a pinch of salt in a rice cooker (or heavy pot). Cook according to rice cooker directions (or set the pot over medium heat for 5 minutes, then turn to low and simmer for 20 minutes). Let stand 10 minutes, then fluff the rice and keep warm.

2 Meanwhile, make the sambal ikan bilis: Heat the oil in a medium skillet over medium heat. Add the anchovies and let them sizzle in the oil, folding them over on themselves until they are a little golden and crisp, about 3 minutes, reducing the heat as necessary so the fish and oil don't burn. Remove the fish with a slotted spoon. Add the shallot to the pan, return the heat to medium, and cook the shallot in the fish oil until wilted and lightly caramelized, about 10 minutes.

3 Return the anchovies to the pan, hold your breath, and stir in the sambal. The initial waft of hot sambal air will catch you off guard if not prepared. Stir in the sugar and lime juice. Remove the mixture from the heat and stir until the sugar is dissolved and you have a chunky, red, sweet, spicy, and fishy sauce. Give it a taste and add a pinch of salt if it needs it.

4 Assemble the dish: Pack a small bowl with coconut rice and invert onto a plate. Surround with quartered eggs, a scoop of sambal ikan bilis, some cucumber slices, and a little pile of peanuts.

This Malaysian breakfast staple is the polar opposite of what most of us break our fast with in the West. But why start your day shoveling in pablum, when you could be playing with the Rubik's Cube of flavor combinations that is nasi lemak? Sambal burns a little; rich coconut rice mollifies. The dish is texture city—crisp cucumbers play off bony little anchovies, softened but still sharp, a sweet–spicy sambal that zaps the zones of the tongue with the finality of the Five Point Palm Exploding Heart Technique. Honestly, it's good for dinner too (most of the time when I make it, it starts as dinner, then once there's sambal ikan bilis around, it's a short path to making it for breakfast).

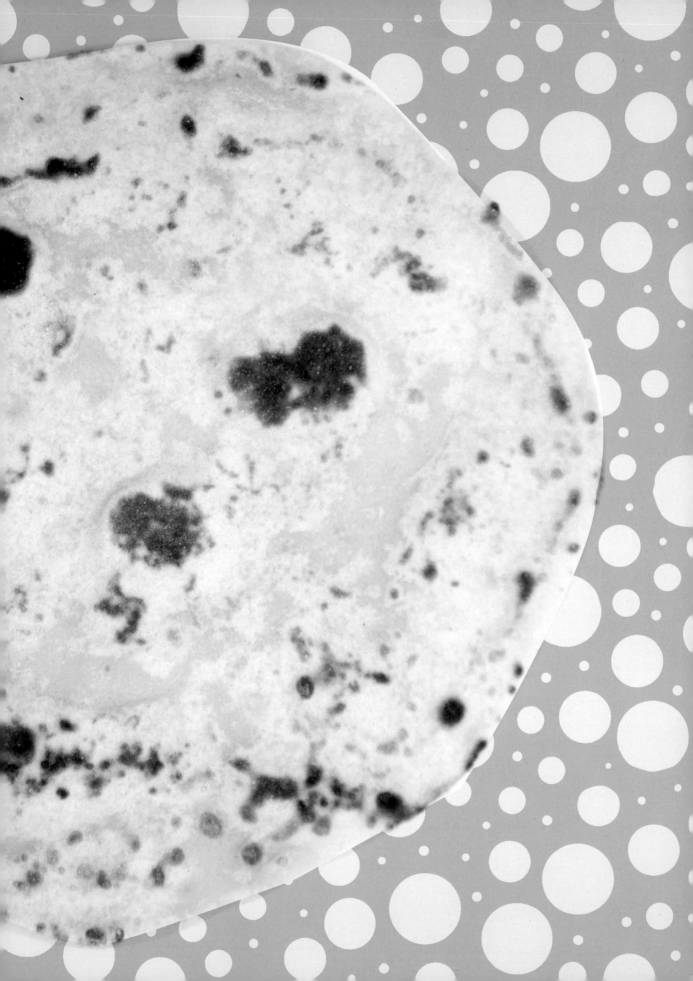

Pancakes

Apam Balik

Pancakes

1⅓ C	all-purpose flour
1⅓ C	rice flour
3 T	cornstarch
2 t	baking powder
½ t	baking soda
¾ C	superfine sugar
½ t	kosher salt
2	large eggs
1 t	vanilla extract
1 C	water
+	melted butter

Filling

+	chopped roasted salted peanuts
+	brown sugar
+	melted butter
+	creamed corn (optional)

1 Make the pancakes: Mix together the flours, cornstarch, baking powder, baking soda, superfine sugar, and salt in a medium bowl. Whisk together the eggs, vanilla, and water in a separate bowl. Pour the wet ingredients into the dry ingredients and whisk until smooth. Cover the batter and chill for at least 1 hour or up to 24 hours.

2 Heat a 6- to 8-inch nonstick pan over medium-low heat. Brush with a little melted butter and pour in ¼ cup of the batter, swirling the pan to create a thin coating over the entire bottom and ½ inch up the sides of the pan. As the batter sets, add a sprinkle of peanuts and brown sugar, a drizzle of melted butter, and a few tablespoons of creamed corn (if using). Fold in half and serve. Repeat with the remaining batter.

This sweet street pancake comes to us from Malaysia via editor Rachel Khong. Apam balik is a rice-flour pancake with creamed corn (!) inside. She says this: "There's a vendor at Tan Jetty in Penang who spoons corn straight from the can into the batter as it is cooking and then deftly extricates the whole thing from the griddle and folds it over like a loose taco, a shape that makes it possible to get both crispy edge and sticky interior in a single bite." With a little time and effort, loose tacos of sweet vegetables can be yours too!

Much of the appeal of apam balik depends on your feelings about creamed corn: You like it, you will like this. You don't? You won't!

Okonomiyaki

Makes 2 large pancakes (4 to 6 servings)

2 C	all-purpose flour
2 t	sugar
1 t	kosher salt
1 t	baking powder
1 C	water
4	large eggs
1 lb	chopped green cabbage (8–10 C)
¼ C	sliced scallions
+	neutral oil
4 oz	cleaned small squid, sliced into tentacles and rings
+	okonomiyaki sauce or barbecue sauce
+	mayonnaise (preferably Kewpie)
+	nori, thinly sliced into confetti
+	katsuobushi (bonito flakes)

1 Whisk together the flour, sugar, salt, and baking powder in a bowl. Add the water and whisk to form a thick pancake batter, then whisk in the eggs until nearly combined but still a little streaky. Add the cabbage and scallions and use your hands to mix—don't overwork the batter, just mix enough to incorporate completely.

2 Heat 1 tablespoon oil in a 10-inch cast iron or nonstick skillet over medium-low heat for a couple of minutes to ensure even heat. Scoop half of the batter into the pan, coaxing it with a spatula into a 1-inch-deep round that does not quite touch the edges of the pan. Scatter half of the squid over the batter and press gently to embed it in the batter.

3 Now comes the tricky part. After about 3 minutes, when the bottom of the pancake is set and light golden brown, use a large spatula to carefully flip it. If your confidence in flipping does not match your lust for squid-and-cabbage pancakes, slide the half-cooked pancake onto a plate, then invert the pan over the plate, and flip the whole thing over, plopping the pancake squid-side down into the pan.

4 Cook the squid side for about 5 minutes, adding a little oil around the sides of the cake if the pan seems dry. Once the squid is cooked and the pancake is nicely browned, flip it again so the squid is facing up. Cook it until the bottom is browned and the pancake is a little puffy and cooked through, 2 to 3 minutes longer.

5 Slide the pancake onto a plate and top with okonomiyaki sauce, mayo, nori, and katsuobushi. Cut into bites and serve hot. Start eating this with friends around the stove while you make the second pancake. Okonomiyaki waits for no one.

***Okonomiyaki* is whatever you want it to be.** It's a blank canvas of a pancake that one condimentizes the bejesus out of; an exaggerated zigzag of two squirt-bottle sauces—Kewpie mayonnaise (which is an eggy-rich MSG-bomb brand of Japanese mayonnaise that comes in a squishy bottle, and which you should certainly seek out if you've never had it), and okonomiyaki sauce, a tangy concoction that's a relation of American-style steak sauces like A1 and Heinz 57. Bonito flakes scattered atop all of this will wriggle with creepy lifelike motion. (The heat of the pancake makes them flutter about; it's a good parlor trick that always surprises the okonomiyaki newbie.)

Squid is a common ingredient in this wildly variable dish—it's cheap and more or less neutral in flavor. Swap out vegetables or other meats for it at will. The cabbage isn't requisite, but I can't imagine okonomiyaki without it.

Scallion Pancakes

Makes 6 pancakes (10 to 12 servings)

4 C	all-purpose flour		**+**	sesame oil (about ½ C)
¼ C	vegetable shortening		**6 T**	minced scallions
+	warm water		**+**	neutral oil
+	kosher salt			

1 Combine 2 cups of the flour with the shortening in a stand mixer fitted with a dough hook. Mix on low speed until the fat is dispersed into a dozen or so nickel-size chunks. Pour 1½ cups warm water into the bowl and mix until a stiff dough forms, about 3 minutes. Stop the mixer and add the remaining 2 cups flour, 2 teaspoons salt, and ⅓ cup water. Knead on medium speed for 3 minutes. The dough will be smooth and supple and hold a fingerprint indefinitely. Wrap the dough in plastic and let rest 10 minutes or refrigerate for up to 2 days.

2 Unwrap the dough and cut it into 6 equal pieces. Roll the pieces into balls and drape with plastic wrap so they don't dry out as you work. Lightly flour your work surface and use a rolling pin to roll one of the balls out into an 8- or 9-inch round. Brush the entire surface of the dough generously with sesame oil and sprinkle with 1 tablespoon scallions. Sprinkle lightly with salt. Now roll the dough into a jelly roll–like log of scallion pancake dough. Form the log into a tight spiral, creating a Cinnabon of scallion pancake dough. Tent with plastic wrap and repeat with the remaining dough, sesame oil, scallions, and salt until you have made 6 Cinnabons. Let them rest at least 10 minutes. (They can also be individually wrapped in plastic and refrigerated for up to 1 day at this point.)

3 Now it is time to flatten the Cinnabons, because you are not making Cinnabons, you are making scallion pancakes. Lightly flour your work surface. Make two or three passes with the rolling pin, gently flattening the disk as you go, then turn it 90 degrees and repeat. Keep going until it's about 8 inches in diameter.

4 Heat ⅛ inch neutral oil in a large skillet over medium heat. Fry the pancakes, flipping once, until very crisp and browned, 5 to 6 minutes total. Cut into wedges and serve hot.

Scallion pancakes are served hot in dim sum restaurants, and will be a popular appetizer in your home, dorm, or commune kitchen. It's nice to put out a little Shanghai-ish dipping sauce for the pancakes if you're so inclined—a 1:1 mixture of soy sauce and Chinkiang vinegar, possibly with some threads of fresh ginger thrown in—though I usually just end up piling it up with sambal oelek (you could use the Super Sauce on page 254, or the stuff that comes with the golden label from Huy Fong foods). This dough, worked in a slightly different fashion, can also profitably be used to ensconce other foods, as demonstrated in the beef roll on page 84.

Beef Roll

Makes 6 rolls

+	**Scallion Pancake dough** (page 82)
+	neutral oil
½ C	hoisin sauce
1 lb	leftover braised beef, thinly sliced, warmed (see disclaimer below)
½ C	roughly chopped cilantro
½ C	sliced scallions, which we left out of the photo but you can add in at home

1 Make the scallion pancake dough, but use melted lard or butter in place of the sesame oil in step 2. Then, in step 3, roll the pancakes out thinner and wider: They should be 10-inch rounds about ⅛ inch thick.

2 To cook these thinner pancakes, rub a medium-hot skillet with an oily paper towel and lay in 1 rolled-out pancake. Cook it until crisp and light golden on both sides, 4 to 5 minutes. You want the pancake to be cooked through, but not as dark and shatteringly crisp as a standard scallion pancake; it needs to still be flexible enough to roll up without breaking.

3 Smear each pancake with some hoisin and top with a layer of beef and a sprinkle of cilantro and scallions. Roll up and slice crosswise into 1-inch bites.

You will often see this called a "Shandong Beef Roll" on menus, an appellation that I don't know to be exactly accurate. This particular rendition came to us through Mary-Frances Heck, who worked on all the recipes for this book, from her friend Brian Tsao, who is a cook in New York and who was born into a Taiwanese restaurant family (that has one restaurant in the states, Mama China, in Las Vegas).

About this pancake, Brian says, "I should also mention they learned a lot of their recipes in the Taiwanese Military Villages that housed hundreds of thousands after the communist takeover of the Mainland. These Military Villages housed people from all regions of the Mainland who were still loyal to Chiang Kai-shek." Which makes us all suspect this dish is one of those serendipities of fusion that result from the chaos of real life instead of one with a neat, pastoral history and clear line back to a particular part of the world.

The wrap is a thinly rolled and lightly browned scallion pancake. The Tsaos use lard in place of the sesame oil that is in our scallion pancake recipe.

MAKE SURE TO READ THIS BEFORE YOU PLAN ON HAVING THIS FOR DINNER TONIGHT: In our fantasy world you would have leftover meat from the Beef Noodle Soup (page 96). In lieu of that, I'd go out there and say it's worth it to braise that beef (it's 2 hours of passive simmering), chill it, and eat it this way the next day. In the spirit of this book's message of peace and easiness: We will admit that we got some good roast beef from a local deli counter and liked that too. Not that we'd tell Grandma Tsao about that.

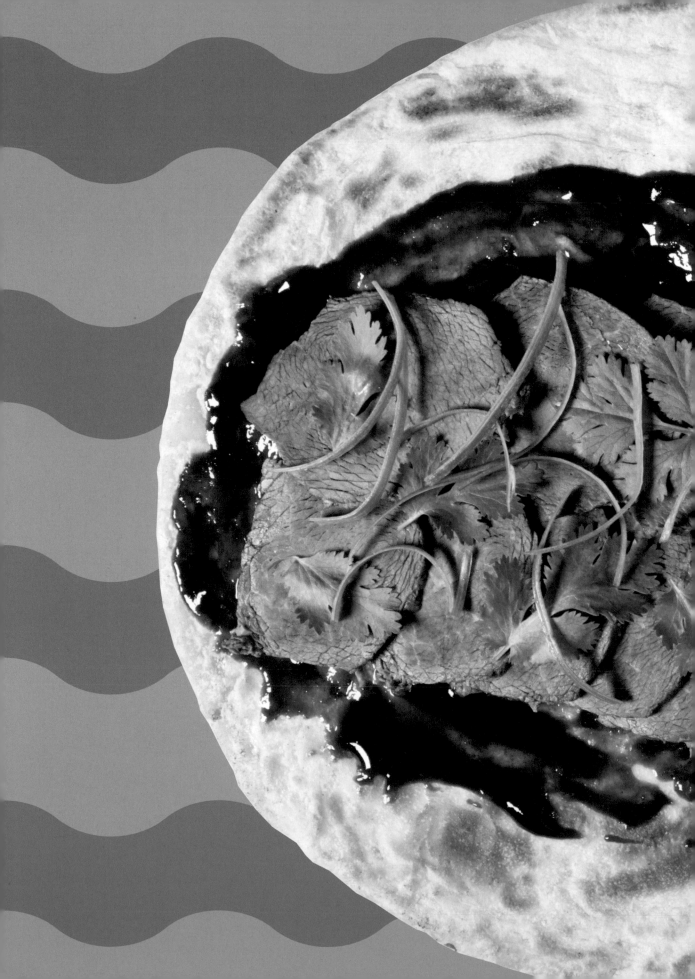

Korean Pumpkin Pancake

Makes 4 to 6 servings

1 lb	pumpkin (or any hard squash, traditionally kabocha), seeded and peeled
1 t	kosher salt
2 T	sugar
½ C	flour
+	neutral oil

1 You need shredded pumpkin. A food processor can make instant work of the gourd; a box grater too, with just a little more elbow grease. If you're a real equipment minimalist, grab a large, sharp knife and cut the pumpkin into manageable hunks, then slice each hunk into thin (⅛-inch) planks. Stack 5 or 6 planks and cut into matchsticks.

2 Toss the pumpkin shreds with the salt and sugar and let stand until the squash has wept several tablespoons of liquid, 15 to 20 minutes. Add the flour, toss, and let stand another 5 minutes for everything to gel.

3 Heat 1 tablespoon oil in a large skillet over medium heat. Working in batches, scoop 2 tablespoons pumpkin mix (or more if you want larger pancakes) into the pan and spread into a ¼-inch-deep layer. Add as many pancakes as will fit comfortably in the pan. Fry, flipping each pancake once, until the pumpkin is tender and the outside is browned and crispy. Repeat with the remaining batter.

Call it a Korean latke. Kabocha squash is standard here, but it can be made with almost any root vegetable. This dish is somewhere between an appetizer and a veg dish to round out a meal. It's not usually served with a dipping sauce, but if you put out a little saucer with a 1:1:1 of soy—rice vinegar—water with a few scallions sliced up in it, I'd probably end up spooning it all over my pancakes because I'm that type of person.

Kimchi Pancake

Makes 1 large pancake, feeds 2 people

1 C	kimchi
¼ C	all-purpose flour
¼ C	rice flour
½ t	kosher salt
¼ C	chopped scallions
+	neutral oil

1 Squeeze the kimchi over a bowl to release as much juice as possible. Top up this liquid with juice from the jar to measure about ½ cup. If you don't have enough juice, add cold water. Roughly chop the kimchi.

2 Whisk together the kimchi juice, flours, and salt. Let stand a couple minutes until slightly thickened. Fold in the kimchi and scallions and let stand a few more minutes until the batter is cohesive.

3 Heat 1 tablespoon oil in a 10-inch skillet over medium-high heat. Dump the batter into the pan and use a spatula to quickly flatten it out into an even, thin round. Cook until the bottom is browned and crispy, 3 to 4 minutes. Flip and cook 2 to 3 minutes longer for the batter to set. Cut into wedges and serve with dipping sauce (see below).

Three things here:
1. Make a few saucers of dipping sauce: Each gets 1 tablespoon each of soy sauce, rice vinegar, and water, and ⅛ teaspoon (a dot or two) of sesame oil. Stir together. Scattering some sesame seeds or the tiniest bit of minced chili over the sauce won't hurt.
2. You need rice flour for this pancake. (Specifically Asian rice flour made from glutinous rice; don't go for the gluten-free health food store stuff.) The mix of flours makes it light and crisp and hard to resist.
3. On account of the irresistibleness, you may want to plan to make an extra one, because it will go fast.

Moo Shu Pancakes

Makes 12 pancakes

2 C	all-purpose flour
¾ C	boiling water
1 T	sesame oil
+	filling, such as **Moo Shu Vegetables** (opposite)
+	hoisin sauce, for serving

1 Place the flour in a large bowl and create a well in the center. Pour the boiling water into the well and begin working the flour into the water with a fork. Once a shaggy dough forms, knead the dough with your hands (remembering that the water was just boiling, so you might have to wait a couple of seconds until the dough is touchable), incorporating any flour that remains at the periphery. Continue kneading the dough in the bowl for 1 minute, then turn onto a work surface and knead for another minute until it's smooth and tender.

2 Roll the dough into a rope about a foot long. Cut into 12 equal pieces and roll each into a smooth ball. It is important for the balls to be the same size, so take your time getting them even and perfectly round.

3 Working with 2 dough balls at a time, brush one side of each with sesame oil. Pick up one piece and flip it onto the other, so the oiled sides are pressed together. Press the dough into a 3-inch patty, applying even pressure to make sure the two halves expand at the same rate and their edges stay even. Using a rolling pin, coax the matched pair into a 6- to 7-inch round, about the width and thickness of a small tortilla. Repeat with the remaining dough balls until you have 6 pancakes.

4 Heat a seasoned cast iron or nonstick skillet over medium-low heat for a couple of minutes. Lay 1 pancake in the pan and cook until the bottom is browned and the top is beginning to show many small or a couple of large bubbles, 2 to 3 minutes. Flip the pancake and cook for about 1 minute, until browned. Remove from the pan and tear apart the two halves to yield 2 pancakes. Stack on a plate and cover with a kitchen towel while cooking the remaining pancakes. Serve with a filling and hoisin.

Picking up the technique of smushing together two dough balls, rolling them out, frying them, then pulling them apart for a moo shu meal is alone worth the price of admission. If you're the sort of snob (like me!) who feels like they've graduated from moo shu meals to more obscure and "authentic" dishes, the deliciousness of this will make you reconsider. I advocate for hoisin as the sauce to marry filling to pancake here, while fully recognizing that plum sauce is what was served at the mall restaurants of my suburban teenage years.

Moo Shu Vegetables

Makes 4 servings

2 T	soy sauce
1 T	Shaoxing wine
½ t	sugar
½ t	cornstarch
+	neutral oil
1 T	chopped fresh ginger
1 T	chopped garlic
1 C	thinly sliced green cabbage
½ C	thinly sliced red cabbage
½ C	thinly sliced red bell pepper
½ C	thinly sliced onion
¼ C	wood ear mushrooms, soaked, drained, and thinly sliced
¼ C	dried lily buds, soaked and drained (optional)
+	**Moo Shu Pancakes** (opposite)
+	hoisin sauce, for serving

1 Stir together the soy sauce, wine, sugar, and cornstarch in a small bowl until the sugar and cornstarch are dissolved. Keep near at hand.

2 Heat a slick of oil in a wok or large heavy skillet over high heat. Add the ginger and garlic and stir-fry for 15 seconds, until aromatic. Add the cabbages, pepper, onion, wood ears, and lilies (if using) and stir-fry until everything is crisp-tender, 3 to 4 minutes.

3 Pour the sauce over the vegetables and fold to coat. When the sauce bubbles and thickens, remove it from the heat. Serve the vegetables with pancakes and hoisin.

Moo Shu
Pancakes
(page 90)
Moo Shu
Vegetables
(page 91)

Soups
and
Stews

Beef Noodle Soup

Makes 4 servings

2 T	neutral oil		1	cinnamon stick (3")
2 lbs	boneless beef shank meat, rinsed and cut into 1" pieces		2 T	Shaoxing wine or dry sherry
			1 T	brown sugar
4 t	kosher salt		1 T	rice vinegar
1½ T	minced fresh ginger		10 C	water
1½ T	minced garlic		1 T	hondashi
1 T	doubanjiang or gochujang (spicy chili-bean paste)		4	baby bok choy, cut in half lengthwise (or use leftover greens)
2 T	soy sauce		8 oz	rice noodles (medium size)
2	whole star anise		⅛ t	sesame oil

1 Heat a Dutch oven over medium–high heat, then coat with the neutral oil. Season the beef with 3 teaspoons of salt. Add the ginger and garlic and stir. After 30 seconds, add the beef and the flavor party—chili-bean paste, soy sauce, star anise, cinnamon, wine, sugar, and vinegar. Stir everything for a minute or so to amalgamate the mess in the pan, then add the water and hondashi and stir to help it dissolve.

2 Bring the pot up to a simmer, then drop the heat to maintain a gentle bubbling simmer. Skim any froth that rises to the surface of the broth in the first 10 minutes, adding a ladleful of water in place of each ladle of fat and scum you remove and discard. Partially cover the pot with a lid and simmer gently until the meat is tender, about 2 hours. At this point the soup can be cooled, covered, and refrigerated for up to 3 days.

3 When you're ready to eat, bring a pot of water to a boil. Blanch the bok choy until just tender—a minute or less—then drain well with a spider and divide among 4 serving bowls. Boil the noodles in the same pot of water according to package directions. Drain and put them in the bowls. Season the broth with the remaining 1 teaspoon salt and the sesame oil, and portion it out over the noodles and greens. Eat hot.

After a few rounds of simplifying this soup, stripping out hours of cooking and different techniques and steps, I was very surprised at just how good it turned out—2 hours of nearly no work can make for a bowl of something that is complex and deep. Taiwanese beef noodle soup was the lodestar for the dish, but we drew in a couple of other influences (like the Japanese instant dashi) to make it delicious and easy. Note that this is a large amount of beef for this amount of soup and will yield some leftovers—making the soup with less meat makes the broth taste meager. These leftovers are what Martha Stewart would call a good thing: The beef is good cold and sliced in a sandwich, or eaten over plain rice with a Super Sauce, and it makes the beef pancake on page 84 stratospherically good.

Rotisserie Chicken Ramen

Makes 4 servings

1	rotisserie chicken, whole or leftover	4	portions ramen noodles (preferably fresh)
4	scallions		
1	piece (1") fresh ginger, thinly sliced	8 t	soy sauce
1	small carrot (optional)	2	cooked eggs (optional but very nice; see **Soy Sauce Eggs,** page 50), halved
1	dried shiitake mushroom		
3	slices bacon (about 2 oz)		
12 C	water		

1 If you're starting with a leftover rotisserie chicken carcass, scavenge it for good meaty bits, and set them aside. If you have purchased a cooked chicken expressly for this recipe, then carefully cut away the breast meat, reserve the drumsticks, and use your fingers to shred off the leg meat—but just the big, fit-for-a-king pieces that come away easily. You can leave plenty of chicken on the carcass; that clingy meat will make for a flavorful soup. Pull or slice the meat into bite-size pieces and reserve in the fridge while you make the broth.

2 Break the chicken carcass into a few pieces and put them in a stockpot. Trim the roots and dark green parts of the scallions and add them to the pot; thinly slice the white and tender green parts and reserve them to garnish the soup. Add the ginger, carrot (if using), shiitake, and bacon. Add the water and bring to a boil. Reduce the heat from a rolling boil to a rollicking simmer, and skim any froth that collects on the surface during the first 10 minutes of simmering.

3 Cook until the liquid is reduced by one-third (to 8 cups), about 2 hours. Strain the broth. (That shiitake is probably pretty delicious and tender at this point so you can save and slice it and use it as a garnish on the finished dish, but scrap the rest.) The broth can be used immediately or refrigerated for up to 2 days.

4 To serve: Bring the broth to a strong simmer and cook the ramen noodles according to package directions. Drain the noodles very well, and portion them out among 4 deep soup bowls. Top with broth. Season each bowl with 2 teaspoons soy sauce, a portion of the reserved chicken meat, scallions, half an egg, and whatever else you've got. (See ideas on the following pages!) Eat immediately.

Do I really have to cook this for TWO HOURS??

We don't want to make you do anything you're not comfortable with. But we found that 2 hours is the sweet spot for flavor extraction and reduction. Also, you don't really do anything during that time except for maybe cook an egg or two—plenty of time to watch an old Eddie Murphy movie or stare endlessly into the antisocial abyss that is your smartphone!

BUT BUT BUT why do I have to skim it?

Skimming the broth during the first 10 minutes will force you to pay attention to the hardness of the simmer, observe the water level in the pot, and get to know the broth.

Also, we found that with rotisserie chicken (unlike plain old raw chicken), there is some rendered grease that can emulsify in a muddy way. Our early stabs at this broth went unskimmed; they came out murky and tasted sort of flat. This approach yields a cleaner-tasting and clearer soup—and a better bowl of ramen.

You don't need more than scallions, an egg, and (in the best case) some meat plundered from the carcass to make a solid serving of soup.

But maybe you've already made this same dish a thousand times and you're looking to spice things up, or maybe you've got a fridge thick with odds and ends. Here are some other things we'd happily throw in the bowl:

Bean sprouts
raw, a handful for
each bowl

Sesame seeds
1 tablespoon
per bowl

Vegetables
The sky is more or less the limit on veggie additions. Your taste will dictate what you wanna plop in your soup. If you're adding something raw at the end as a topping—let's say napa cabbage because it's easy to have extra—make sure to cut it thin enough that the heat of the soup can cook it, and in a shape that will make it nice to eat along with the noodles (i.e., a chiffonade). Do not add leftover vegetables cold from the fridge—that's like adding an ice cube to a hot cup of coffee. Heat 'em up first!

Other meats
Try shredded pork shoulder or any nubbins of tasty roasted or grilled meat.

Menma
Menma are cured bamboo shoots often served in ramen. Some Japanese markets carry these, and if you find a shelf-stable version intended to be eaten without any additional preparation, they're worth keeping in the pantry.

Nori
1 torn-up sheet per bowl

Togarashi
classic Japanese hot pepper powder to spike a bowl

Chicken Noodle Soup

Makes 4 servings

1	whole chicken (3–4 lbs)		**¼ t**	coriander seeds
8 C	water, or more as needed		**¼ t**	black peppercorns
½ C	sliced carrot		**1 t**	Sichuan peppercorns
1 C	sliced onion		**1**	bay leaf
2	scallions		**2 t**	soy sauce
2	slices (¼" thick) fresh ginger		**¼ t**	freshly ground black pepper
1 t	kosher salt		**8 oz**	Pennsylvania Dutch egg noodles
4	garlic cloves		**+**	garnishes: thinly sliced scallions,
1	point star anise			cilantro, chili oil, etc.

1 Place the chicken, breast-side down, in a stockpot and cover with the water by 1 inch. Set the pot over medium–high heat and bring to a boil, then reduce to a simmer, skimming the froth that collects on the surface of the broth during the first 10 minutes. Add the remaining ingredients through the bay leaf, and cover the pot. Simmer for 5 minutes longer and remove from the heat. Let the broth steep, covered and unbothered, for 45 minutes.

2 Carefully remove the chicken from the pot to a carving board (a cutting board with a moat!) or a plate. Strain the broth (discarding the rest of the solids). Wipe the pot clean, add back the strained broth, and bring to a simmer. Bring a separate pot of salted water to a boil for the noodles.

3 When the chicken is cool enough to handle, pull the meat from the carcass and shred it into bite-size pieces (discard the skin and bones). Transfer the chicken to a small bowl and season the meat with soy sauce and pepper.

4 Cook the noodles according to package directions. Drain well and portion out among 4 serving bowls. Top each with hot broth, then with seasoned chicken and desired garnishes. Serve hot.

Steeping meat like tea is a favorite technique for flavor extraction at *Lucky Peach* HQ. Here we use it to make a pot of flavorful chicken broth without drying out the meat of the bird, which we then pick and season and serve on top of the soup. We've outlined the most basic bowl possible—we even used Dutch egg noodles, which you can find in even the most poorly provisioned doomsday bunker, though you are welcome to swap literally any other noodle in their place. See our ideas on pages 100 and 101 (following Rotisserie Chicken Ramen) for other ways to trick out this soup.

Miso Clam Chowder

Makes 4 servings

2 T	unsalted butter
4	scallions, thinly sliced, whites and greens separated
2	garlic cloves, minced
1	bay leaf
1 T	thyme leaves
2 C	clam juice or water
8 oz	red potatoes, cut into ½" pieces
16	littleneck clams, scrubbed
2 T	red miso
½ C	heavy cream
+	sea salt and freshly ground black pepper
+	optional garnishes: cilantro, a few drops of fish sauce, lime, white pepper, crisp bacon lardons

1 Melt the butter in a medium saucepan over medium heat. Add the scallion whites and garlic and sauté until softened, about 4 minutes. Add the bay leaf, thyme, clam juice, and potatoes. Bring to a simmer, cover, and cook until the potatoes are tender, about 20 minutes.

2 Add the clams, cover, and simmer gently until the clams open, about 5 minutes. Remove from the heat.

3 Measure the miso into a small bowl and add a ladleful of the hot clam broth. Knead the miso with the back of a spoon until it dissolves into the broth, then pour the liquid back into the pan along with the cream. Season with salt to taste and a generous amount of black pepper and stir in the scallion greens. Divide among 4 serving bowls and garnish as you see fit.

The more "Asian" point of view would be to say that adding clams to dashi makes a great soup (it does) or that adding clams to miso soup makes a great soup better (also true). But since cross-cultural co-option is a two-way street, how about this: Miso makes a classic Boston clam chowder even better.

Doenjang Jigae

Makes 4 servings

4 C	water
2 T	hondashi
3 T	doenjang or miso
1 C	pieces (½") bacon (optional but recommended)
1 C	pieces (¾") potato (about 1 large waxy potato)
1	large onion, cut into 1" pieces (about 1½ C)
1	medium zucchini, cut into ½" rounds
1	container (14 oz) firm tofu, cut into 1" pieces
5	garlic cloves, sliced thin
2 C	button mushrooms, quartered
1	jalapeño, sliced into rings
2	scallions, thinly sliced (about ½ C)
+	cooked short- or medium-grain rice, for serving

1 Combine the water, hondashi, doenjang, bacon (if using), potato, and onion in a heavy 2-quart saucepan. Bring to a simmer over medium heat, then reduce the heat and cook gently until the flavor of bacon is infused into the soup and the potatoes are halfway cooked, about 10 minutes.

2 Stir in the zucchini, tofu, garlic, mushrooms, and jalapeño. Simmer until the potatoes and zucchini are completely tender, about 15 minutes. Stir in the scallions and serve with rice.

Doenjang jigae is elemental Korean comfort food, a one-pot stew of pure home comfort. Tony Kim of the Momofuku restaurants described it as kind of like stone soup—with a little doenjang or miso and some kind of meat or protein (we call for bacon here, but it could be any pork, or even clams). You've got the base, then you add the vegetables you can scrounge to fortify and round it out. Every version of it I've ever seen has had zucchini in it, regardless of the setting it was served in, home or restaurant, or the season it was cooked in. The why behind that escapes me.

Slow Cooker Pho

Makes 4 servings

1	large yellow onion, sliced into ½" rounds
1	piece (2") fresh ginger, halved lengthwise
1 t	neutral oil
2 lbs	chuck short ribs
+	kosher salt
2	whole star anise
1	cinnamon stick (3")
4	whole cloves
8 C	beef broth
1–2 T	fish sauce
10 oz	flat rice noodles, fettuccine-size

Garnishes

1 C	bean sprouts
½ C	Thai basil leaves
½ C	mint leaves
½ C	cilantro, stems and leaves
2	jalapeños, sliced into ¼" rounds
+	lime wedges
+	hoisin sauce, sriracha, or sambal

1 Heat the broiler. Line a baking sheet with foil.

2 Arrange the onion slices and ginger on the baking sheet pan and brush with the oil. Broil until charred in spots, about 10 minutes.

3 Season the short ribs with salt. Arrange the onions and ginger, short ribs, star anise, cinnamon, cloves, and beef broth in a large slow cooker. Cover and cook on high for 4 hours, or until the meat is just tender. Turn off the slow cooker and let the broth and meat rest for 30 minutes. Remove the meat from the broth and slide off the bones. Strain the broth (discard the solids). Skim any fat that rises to the surface of the broth. (At this point, the broth and meat can be refrigerated for up to 3 days. Rewarm before proceeding.)

4 Return the broth to a simmer and season with the fish sauce and salt.

5 Meanwhile, prepare the rice noodles according to package directions. Drain well.

6 Slice the meat into bite–size pieces. Portion out the noodles and meat among 4 large soup bowls. Ladle the hot broth into the bowls, warming the noodles and meat. Serve with the garnishes.

I am against the use of packaged broth. I think it's gross, and I think it's easy enough to make your own at home—what I do is roast off some cheap cut from the butcher shop, throw it in a pot with water, simmer (or simmer/steep like in the Chicken Noodle Soup, page 102), strain, and freeze it. For the most part, we have avoided calling for packaged broth in this book. But tension between belief and desire arose when we were working on this pho recipe, which I wanted because New York is a pho desert. (Yes, there are okay bowls here and there, but nothing to compare with what can be got in Oklahoma City or New Orleans, to say nothing of the greater Los Angeles area. Or Toronto. But I digress.) Homemade beef broth really brings this bowl over the top, but it also probably disqualifies it from being easy. Do what you think is right.

Of course, co-editor Dave Chang protested this recipe on different grounds: "Why make pho? Why go through the trouble? Why not just dump a shot of amaro in the beef noodle soup?"

Hot and Sour Soup

Makes 4 servings

½ C	wood ear mushrooms
2 T	neutral oil
1 T	chopped garlic
1 T	chopped fresh ginger
½ C	chopped scallions
8 oz	pork shoulder, cut into fat matchsticks (1" long, ¼" wide)
4 C	chicken broth
8 oz	soft tofu, cut into ½" cubes
1 t	sugar
½ C	rice vinegar
3 T	soy sauce
1 t	freshly ground black pepper
1 t	sesame oil
1 T	sriracha, or more to taste
2	large eggs (optional)

1 Cover the mushrooms with warm water and soak until plump and pliable, about 30 minutes. Drain and set aside.

2 Heat the neutral oil in a large heavy saucepan over medium heat. Add the garlic, ginger, scallions, and pork and cook, stirring, until the aromatics soften and the pork whitens, about 4 minutes. Pour in the broth and bring to a simmer.

3 Stir in the tofu, sugar, vinegar, soy sauce, pepper, sesame oil, and sriracha. Return to a simmer and adjust the seasoning. (Some of us like as much as an additional ⅓ cup vinegar to really up the sour.)

4 If using the eggs, beat them in a small bowl and drizzle over the soup while gently stirring. When the eggs set into strands, divide the soup among 4 bowls and serve.

Most of my life's admittedly limited experiences with hot 'n' sour soup were beyond discouraging: a viscous liquid, stingily sour, unexcitingly spiced. As such, I was dead set against it going in this book, crotchety and disagreeable.

But in an act of hounding worthy of Sam-I-Am, I was argued down, and proved wrong with this rendition, cribbed from the pages of *Flour, Too*, a cookbook by the eminent Bostonian chef Joanne Chang. I ate it hot, two pints straight out of the pot. I ate it cold, later that night, straight from the fridge. I have not had the opportunity to take it with a goat, in a boat, or whatever else the guy in the book does, but like him, I am now fully down to clown.

Massaman Curry

Makes 4 to 6 servings

1	stalk lemongrass		1	cinnamon stick (3")
2 T	neutral or coconut oil		1	can (14 oz) coconut milk
1	small onion, chopped		2 C	water
2 T	minced garlic		1½ lbs	chicken thighs
2 T	minced fresh ginger		2 t	kosher salt
¼ C	red curry paste		1 lb	Yukon Gold potatoes
1 t	ground coriander		½ C	roasted unsalted peanuts
½ t	turmeric		1 T	fish sauce
3	whole star anise		1–2 T	lime juice
2	kaffir lime leaves (optional, but very nice if you can find them!)		+	palm or brown sugar
			+	cooked rice, for serving

1 Smash the lemongrass with the back of a knife at ½-inch intervals, then bend the stalk and tie it into a knot. This will help release the flavor in the lemongrass.

2 Heat the oil in a large Dutch oven over medium heat. Add the onion, garlic, and ginger and sweat until aromatic and softened, about 5 minutes. Add the curry paste, coriander, and turmeric and stir to coat the vegetables in the paste. Once incorporated, toss in the star anise, lime leaves (if using), cinnamon, and lemongrass. Stir in the coconut milk and water and bring to a simmer. Add the chicken and simmer, uncovered, for 20 minutes. Add the potatoes and peanuts and cook until tender, about 25 minutes longer.

3 Remove the star anise, cinnamon, lime leaves, and lemongrass and discard. At this point the curry may be cooled and refrigerated for up to 2 days. (Reheat over medium-low heat, stirring frequently to avoid scorching.)

4 Stir the fish sauce and lime juice into the curry, then adjust the seasoning with sugar and salt. Serve with rice.

Curry paste is hard to argue with: The stuff is delicious, and it's always smart to have a jar or a can in the pantry. While it can carry the day on its own, why not make it part of a coalition of the willing to make dinner even more flavorful? Hence this spiced-up base—bolstered by star anise, cinnamon, coriander, and turmeric, along with lemongrass and kaffir lime leaves (if you can find them)—which gets you into bona fide Massaman territory, and pretty easily too. String up a Mission Accomplished banner over the finished dish.

Soy-Braised Short Ribs

Makes 6 servings

1 C	chopped Asian pear or 1 C apple juice
1 C	mirin
½ C	sugar
1 C	soy sauce
1	head garlic, cloves smashed and peeled
1	bunch scallions
6 lbs	bone-in short ribs
1 lb	carrots, cut into chunks
1 lb	baby potatoes
1 t	sesame oil
+	freshly ground black pepper
+	cooked short-grain rice, for serving

1 Combine the pear, mirin, sugar, soy sauce, garlic, and scallions in a large Dutch oven. Arrange the short ribs meat-side down in the liquid and add water to cover. Set the pot over medium-high heat and bring to a simmer. Reduce the heat as needed to maintain a very gentle simmer and cook, partially covered, flipping and rotating the ribs occasionally, until bouncy-tender, about 2 hours. At this point, you can cool the contents of the pot and refrigerate for up to 3 days.

2 Remove the ribs from their braising liquid and skim any fat from the surface. If the liquid has gelled, you'll need to warm it briefly, so that you can strain out the now-spent aromatics. Return the ribs and liquid to the pot, add the carrots and potatoes, and cook uncovered until tender, 20 to 25 minutes. Stir in the sesame oil and season with pepper. Serve with short-grain rice.

Lucky Peach **editor Dave Chang is known for his love of cheap beer,** his pork buns, and his rage. But if you wanna see childlike delight overtake him, all you need to do is talk to him about his mom's braised short ribs, which are the inspiration for this dish.

Hot Pot Party Town

I think my wife and I first acquired our hot plate—a $9.99 electric burner—during a gas outage that neutered our stove and our ability to make dinner for ourselves. I remember waiting for a pot of water to boil on it being approximately as interminable as a bad acid trip at the DMV, and accordingly planned all future use of it to be for meek heating needs. Still, we stuck it in a closet, figuring at some point the robust network of century-old pipes that power the metropolis would give out again, and we'd come calling for it.

And of course that did happen, but in the intervening years we tried to find a way to make this otherwise underwhelming piece of kitchen equipment part of our lives. The answer: hot pot. There are bladders of just-add-water Sichuan hot pot stuff at most big Chinese markets, and I like them, but they taste weird and have ingredient lists that are confusing and morally troubling. We do *shabu-shabu* and other meat-based hot pot–type things because there's a Japanese butcher shop a few hundred yards from my front door that specializes in the super-thin sliced meat that you need for swishing around in hot pots. If you don't have access to it—and most people in most places don't—meat-based hot pots are gonna be too sinewy to be fun.

But this here hot pot, it's a different story! No creepy bagged broth. No fancy meat needed. Sure there are a few elements to pull together, and a random piece of kitchen equipment called for. But with an extension cord and a bunch of little dishes to dole out sauces in, it's an easy path to Party Town, which is a fine place to find oneself. It is easy to scale up or down—use more or less of whatever you like. Cut everything up nicely—the tofu into 1-inch blocks, the greens into attractive bites. Pile it onto a platter. Make sure that the hot pot is within everybody's reach, and your work is done.

Tofu in
Kombu Dashi
Hot Pot
(page 118)

Tofu in Kombu Dashi Hot Pot

Makes 4 servings

2	pieces (6") kombu
+	sauces: soy sauce, **Sesame Dipping Sauce** (opposite), and **Ponzu** (opposite); **Carrot-Ginger Dressing** (page 248) or **Odd Flavor Sauce** (page 258) would also be welcome
+	**Kabocha Rice** (page 146)
3	scallions, thinly sliced
1	piece (2") fresh ginger, grated
1	sheet nori, slivered or crumbled
24 oz	best-quality firm tofu (about 1½ blocks), cut into 1" cubes
2	large bunches (3–4 lbs) greens (such as broccoli rabe, broccolini, mustard greens, mizuna, or baby bok choy), cut into bite-size pieces

1 Fill a shallow, wide pot one-third of the way full with cold water and add the kombu. Bring to a gentle simmer on a hot plate in the center of the dinner table.

2 Pour the sauces into little dipping bowls for each diner. Everyone should get a saucer of soy. Divide the kabocha rice among bowls for your guests to eat over.

Put out the scallions, grated ginger, and nori—guests can add them to their meal as they go.

3 Gather around the hot pot. Add the tofu and greens and let them cook to taste—wilted or just warmed through, it's up to you. Employ sauces and seasonings at will.

Sesame Dipping Sauce

Makes ½ cup

¼ C	tahini
1 T	soy sauce
1 T	mirin
1 t	rice vinegar
½ t	sesame oil
2 T	water

Mix all the ingredients in a bowl. If needed, thin with additional water to a honey-like consistency.

Ponzu

Makes 1 cup

½ C	soy sauce
2 T	fresh lemon juice
6 T	fresh tangerine juice

Combine the soy sauce, lemon juice, and tangerine juice in a nonreactive container and stir to combine. Cover and refrigerate for up to 1 month.

This bootleg ponzu is stolen from Nancy Singleton Hachisu's *Japanese Farm Food,* a wonderful reference for homey, seasonal Japanese cooking ideas. Ponzu is:

1. Traditionally made with yuzu and/or sudachi (two kinds of Japanese citrus), but you can sub in tangerine and lemon to similar effect.

2. Purchasable. Bottled ponzu can be okay to great.

3. Also lovely with simply grilled or broiled fish.

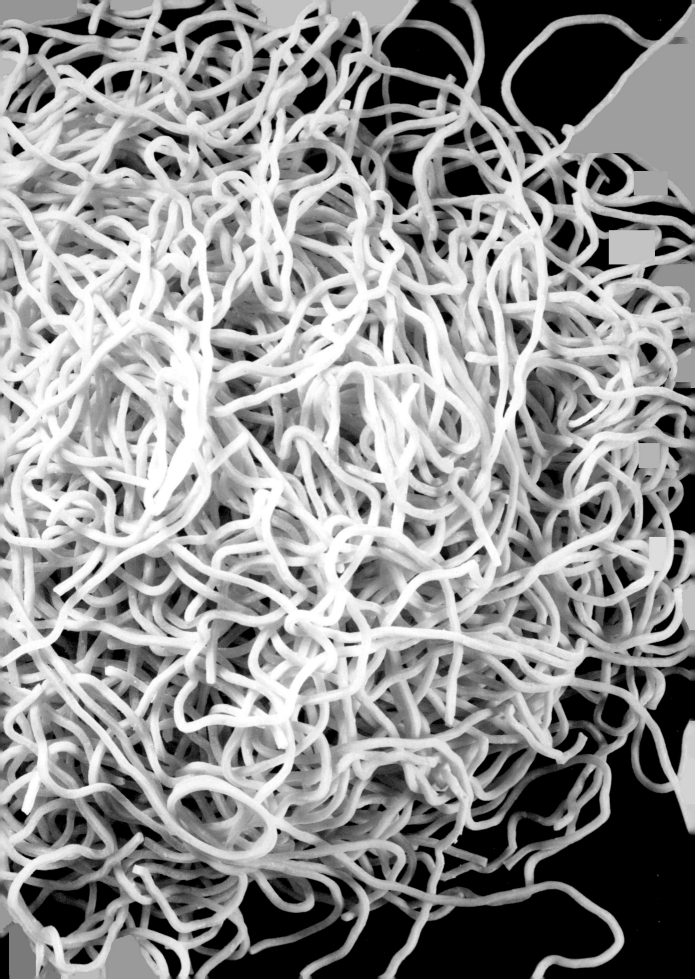

Noodles

Economy Noodles

Makes 2 servings

4 oz	rice vermicelli
1 T	canola oil
2	garlic cloves, minced
3 T	soy sauce
2 t	fish sauce
1½ t	sugar
1 C	bean sprouts
+	white pepper

1 Prepare the noodles according to package directions, which likely means "soak in hot water." Drain and set aside.

2 Heat the oil in a wok or 12-inch cast iron skillet set over high heat until shimmering. Add the garlic and cook for a minute until fragrant. Remove from the heat and stir in the soy sauce, fish sauce, and sugar until the sugar dissolves.

3 Return the pan to the heat, add the bean sprouts, and stir-fry for 1 minute. Add the noodles and cook, tossing them until they absorb the sauce and are heated through. Finish with a couple grinds of white pepper.

The "economy" of these noodles is easy to understand: There's almost nothing in them and it takes almost nothing to putting them together, but they're delicious enough to be a streetside staple in Malaysia. The real fun starts when you build on this recipe. Add a fried egg! Add leftover steak! Or Chinese sausage or whatever protein or vegetable seems like it'd be good with a bowl of noodles.

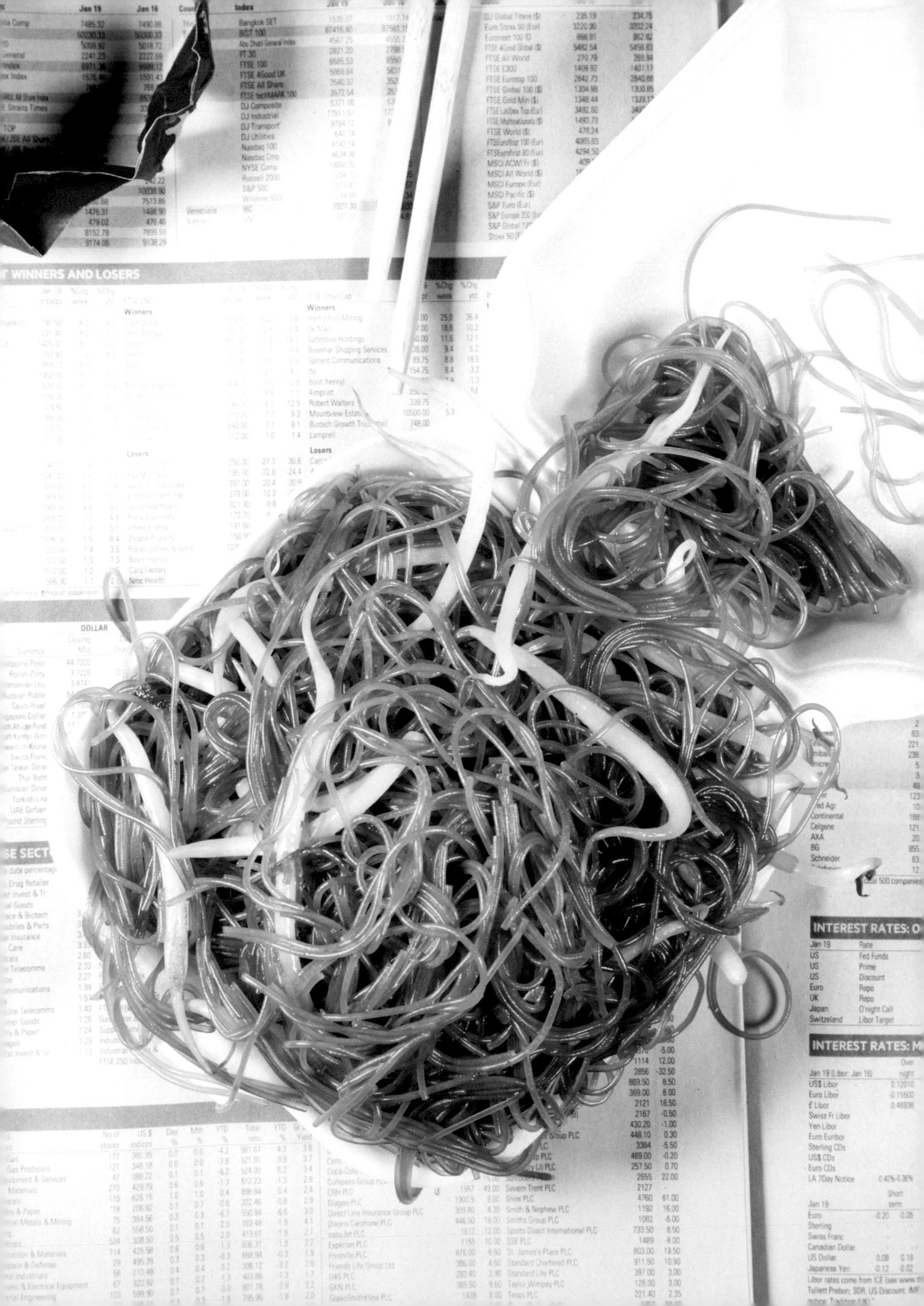

WINNERS AND LOSERS
Winners
Losers
DOLLAR
INTEREST RATES:

Cold Soba with Mushrooms and Leek

Makes 4 servings

1	package (300 g/10.5 oz) soba noodles
1	medium leek, dark green tops trimmed off
1 T	neutral oil (or half neutral oil and half chili oil, if you want it spicy)
4 oz	fresh shiitake mushrooms, stems discarded, caps sliced
¼ C	**Kaeshi** (opposite), or more to taste
1 T	hondashi dissolved in 4 C hot water (or use **Dashi,** page 73)

1 Set up a large bowl of ice and water. Bring a large pot of water to a boil. Cook the soba noodles until just softened but not yet slack, 2 to 3 minutes. Drain and shock in the ice water, agitating the noodles with your hand to help the noodles cool as quickly as possible. Drain well and portion among 4 serving dishes.

2 Halve the trimmed leek lengthwise and rinse in cold water. Cut the leek crosswise into 3-inch sections, then slice lengthwise into matchsticks.

3 Heat a wok or cast iron skillet over medium-high heat, coat with the oil, and stir-fry the leek until it's browned, 5 to 7 minutes. Add the mushrooms and cook until soft. Then add enough kaeshi to moisten the vegetables, about ¼ cup. When the mixture starts to bubble, turn off the heat and add the hondashi. Divide among 4 side bowls. Serve at once, dipping the cold soba into the hot broth. Slurp heartily.

Soba culture in Japan is a borderline mystical practice. Chefs spend their whole lives making noodles and broth day in and day out, practicing *kaizen*—the belief that focus and repetition leads to improvement, maybe even micro-improvements, in the quality of the finished product.

This recipe is not about that. It's about nights when you need dinner on the table, a dish that's light enough to feel supermodel-y but also satisfying enough that you won't raccoon-raid the ice cream supply right after. This is one of the few recipes in this book that calls for a secondary recipe, but the kaeshi is an ease-maker for anybody who wants to eat soba on the regular. The 10 minutes it takes to make will translate into a year's worth of practically instant soba meals. Also, the eagle-eyed among you will note a fresh wasabi root loitering in the back of this photo. Fresh wasabi is expensive and has to be mail-ordered from the Pacific Northwest (at least in America, and assuming you don't live next door to a wasabi farm), but a little grated into your dipping sauce is a luxurious bump-up to the dish.

Kaeshi

Makes 3+ cups

½ C	mirin
1¼ C	sugar
2 C	soy sauce

1 Bring the mirin to a simmer in a small saucepan over high heat. Cook, stirring constantly, until you no longer smell alcohol, 3 to 5 minutes.

2 Stir in the sugar and continue cooking and stirring until the sugar has dissolved. Add the soy sauce and watch as the kaeshi heats up and comes almost to a boil. You will see tiny bubbles form on the perimeter— remove the pan from the heat as soon as the entire surface of the kaeshi becomes creamy tan from minute bubbles. Cool, decant into a jar with a tight-fitting lid, and store for up to 1 year in the fridge.

Jap Chae

Makes 8 servings

10 oz	cellophane or sweet potato noodles
2 T	grapeseed oil
3 C	thinly sliced red onions (1 large or 2 small)
3 C	thinly sliced red bell peppers (2 peppers)
+	kosher salt and freshly ground black pepper
1 C	julienned carrot (1 large)
4 C	thinly sliced shiitake mushroom caps (about 8 oz)
1	bunch scallions, cut into 1" pieces (about 4 oz)
2 T	minced garlic
½ C	mirin
½ C	soy sauce
2 t	sugar
1½ t	sesame oil
3 T	toasted sesame seeds

1 Set up a large bowl of ice and water. Bring a large pot of water to a boil. Cook the noodles according to package directions. Drain the noodles, shock in the ice water, and drain again. Using kitchen scissors, cut the noodles a couple of times to break up the long strands, then transfer to a large bowl.

2 Heat the grapeseed oil in a large skillet over medium heat. Add the onion and bell peppers and cook until the vegetables have softened but still retain their crunch. Season with salt and pepper. Add the carrots, shiitakes, scallions, and garlic and cook until the vegetables are a soft, lightly caramelized mass, about 10 minutes longer.

3 Deglaze the pan with the mirin, using a spatula to scrape up any stuck-on bits from the bottom of the pan.

4 Add the vegetables to the bowl of noodles. Stir in the soy sauce, sugar, sesame oil, and sesame seeds and toss to combine. Season to taste with salt and pepper. Serve at room temperature on a large platter.

Sturdy noodles, heavily seasoned, at room temperature, with enough stuff tossed in there to be almost pasta salad–y—I can't say the promise of jap chae comes through on paper. But the truth is in the eating. I like jap chae best as a side dish, with a big Korean spread; failing that, serve it with kimchi on the side.

Pad See Ew

8 oz	boneless, skinless chicken thighs, thinly sliced crosswise
¼ C	oyster sauce
2 T	soy sauce
2 T	rice vinegar
1 T	sugar
2 T	neutral oil
2	garlic cloves, thinly sliced
5	stalks Chinese broccoli or broccoli rabe, chopped
2	large eggs, beaten
8 oz	fresh wide rice noodles
+	kosher salt and white pepper
+	lime wedges, for serving

1 Mix the chicken with the oyster sauce in a small bowl and set aside. Stir together the soy sauce, vinegar, and sugar in another small bowl and set aside.

2 Set a wok or large skillet over high heat and coat with the oil. After a minute, add the garlic and broccoli and stir-fry until the broccoli is bright green and crisp-tender, 1 to 2 minutes. Transfer to a plate.

3 Add the chicken and oyster sauce to the wok and stir-fry until the chicken is just cooked through, about 3 minutes.

Transfer to the plate with the broccoli.

4 Add the egg to the wok and cook without stirring for 5 seconds, stir, chop into large curds, and cook until just set, about 30 seconds longer. Toss in the noodles and stir-fry until heated through. Return the broccoli and chicken to the pan and add the sauce. Cook, stirring, until everything is sizzling and steaming and heated through. Season to taste with salt and white pepper. Serve with lime wedges.

The Internet, as you well know, is propped up by two things: pornography and easy renditions of pad Thai. Neither simulacrum is as satisfying as the real thing.

Pad see ew, on the other hand, is naturally easy, a crowd-pleasing knockout that survives translation into a lazy-quick preparation like this one.

You can scale this dish up, but cook it in batches that fit your wok and serve portions as they are ready. If your friends or family complain that they all want to eat at the same time, yell at them loudly in Thai and tell them that you haven't dedicated your life to selling this dish on the side of the street just to pile a bunch of noodles up in a wok and let them get gummy and underflavored. Then charge them extra. Tourists never calculate the exchange rate of the *baht* fast enough.

128

Pesto Ramen

Makes 4 servings

4 C	basil leaves
1 T	pine nuts
1	garlic clove
½ C	olive oil
+	kosher salt
1 T	grated parmesan
1 T	grated pecorino Romano, plus more for garnish
4	portions fresh ramen noodles

1 Wash the basil, leaving some water clinging to the leaves. Roughly chop the pine nuts, garlic, and olive oil in a blender or food processor. With the motor running, add the basil and a pinch of salt and process until smooth. Add the parmesan and pecorino and pulse to mix.

2 Bring a large pot of salted water to a boil. Cook the noodles until they are relaxed but firmer than al dente, about 2 minutes—they will continue to soften after coming out of the water. Drain, rinse quickly in cold water, and toss in a bowl with the pesto. Top with a sprinkle of pecorino and serve.

Before Danny Bowien was famous for cooking "Americanized Oriental Cuisine" at Mission Chinese Food, he worked for a Ligurian chef in San Francisco. Through some impossible-sounding fable of a story, he ended up competing in an international pesto-making competition and winning, this Korean kid from Oklahoma beating the Italians at their own game. As an accredited pesto master, he is sometimes disposed to make the green sauce during the months when basil is in high stride. This led, for a brief few nights at the cramped little space that was the first iteration of Mission Chinese Food New York, to pesto ramen. It sounds insane, of course, but it is mega delicious, possibly better than pesto on pasta, and easy to boot. Fresh ramen noodles are a must for this dish. We like Sun Noodle, which probably sells fresh ramen somewhere near your ZIP code.

Hiyashi Somen

Makes 4 servings

2 t	hondashi dissolved in 2 C hot water (or use **Dashi,** page 73)
½ C	soy sauce
2 T	mirin
2 T	sugar
1 T	dried baby shrimp (optional)
+	kosher salt
1	package (300 g/10.5 oz) somen
2	scallions, finely sliced
+	wasabi paste (optional)

1 Combine the hondashi, soy sauce, mirin, sugar, and dried shrimp (if using) in a small saucepan. Cook, stirring, over medium heat, just until the sugar is dissolved. Strain the dipping sauce into another container to cool (you want it to be between ice-cold and room temperature). Discard the shrimp.

2 Bring a large pot of salted water to a boil. Drop in the somen and cook until tender, 2 to 4 minutes. Drain and rinse the noodles in a colander under cold running water.

3 Serve each guest a small bowl of noodles twisted into a little nest on top of a couple ice cubes alongside a small bowl with ½ cup of the dipping sauce scattered with the sliced scallions. Pass around a little dish of wasabi, if desired, to stir into the dipping sauce.

When it is hot, dog-days hot, and sitting near an open window feels like sticking your head in an oven, this is what you want to eat. You can top hiyashi somen with nothing, or you can top it with what's in your fridge. For example, we like a soupçon of nori chiffonade, a julienne of raw cucumbers, and/or egg ribbons (beaten eggs cooked into a flat little crepe, and then cut into thin ribbons).

"Asian" "Ragus"

Spicy Mushroom Ragu
(page 137)

In the house I was raised in, there was one kind of noodle—Italian pasta—and one kind of sauce that went on it: a ground–beef–and–tomato ragu that simmered for hours and hours. I still love it. Everybody, kind of literally everybody, from Shanghai to St. Louis, loves that kind of Italian/Italian–American cooking.

But what about the ragus of Asia? Surely Chinese and Korean *nonnas* like to simmer their sauces on Sunday too, thus making dinner later in the week as easy as boiling up some noodles.

We whittled our way down to these three favorites.

**Sichuan
Pork Ragu**
(page 136)

**Sichuanese
Chopped
Celery
with Beef**
(page 138)

Sichuan Pork Ragu

Makes about 1 quart (4 servings with noodles or rice)

2 T	neutral oil
2	large yellow onions, halved and thinly sliced (about 5 C)
1 lb	ground pork
1 T	chopped garlic
2 T	doubanjiang or gochujang (spicy chili-bean paste)
1 T	Sichuan peppercorns
1 t	chili flakes (preferably gochugaru)
1 T	soy sauce
1 T	sugar
¼ C	water
+	kosher salt
2 C	coarsely chopped bok choy
+	cooked fresh wheat noodles (lo mein or ramen), rice noodles, spaghetti, or rice if that's what you feel like having
+	thinly sliced scallions, for garnish

1 Heat 1 tablespoon oil in a 3-quart saucepan (or a wide deep skillet) over medium heat. Add the onions and cook, stirring and folding, until the onions are light golden but still retain their shape, about 15 minutes. Scoop the onions onto a plate and wipe out the skillet with a towel.

2 Heat the remaining 1 tablespoon oil in the pan, then add the ground pork and cook, breaking the meat into small pieces with a spoon, until just cooked through, about 8 minutes.

3 Push the meat to one side of the pan and add the garlic to the pork drippings. Sweat until fragrant, 1 to 2 minutes, then remove from the heat. Stir in the chili-bean paste, peppercorns, chili flakes, soy sauce, sugar, water, and reserved onions. Season to taste with salt. At this point, the sauce may be refrigerated or frozen. Reheat before proceeding.

4 Bring the sauce to a simmer over medium heat and stir in the chopped greens. Cook, stirring occasionally, until the stems are just tender, 3 to 5 minutes. Serve the sauce over noodles or rice, sprinkled with scallions.

This bastard love child of Bolognese and mapo tofu is a de-escalated and simplified version of a dish from Momofuku Ssäm Bar. You will Win Friends and Influence People by serving it in your home.

Spicy Mushroom Ragu

Makes about 1 quart (6 to 8 servings with noodles or rice)

8 oz	fresh shiitake or button mushrooms, stems discarded
2	small carrots, roughly chopped
1	small onion, roughly chopped
4 oz	takuan (pickled daikon) or canned Sichuan pickled radish, chopped
10	garlic cloves, roughly chopped
½ C	canola oil
1 t	kosher salt
½ t	chili flakes
⅓ C	gochujang or doubanjiang (spicy chili-bean paste)
2 T	fermented black beans
¼ C	soy sauce
+	cooked fresh wheat noodles (lo mein or ramen), rice noodles, spaghetti, or rice if that's what you feel like having

1 Combine the mushrooms, carrots, onion, takuan, and garlic in a food processor and pulse to finely chop.

2 Heat the oil in a large Dutch oven over medium heat. Add the chopped vegetables and salt. Cook until softened, about 20 minutes.

3 Stir in the chili flakes, gochujang, black beans, and soy sauce. Simmer, uncovered, over low heat, stirring frequently to prevent scorching, until all the liquid has evaporated, about 30 minutes. At this point, the sauce may be refrigerated or frozen. Reheat before proceeding. Serve over noodles or rice.

Dave Chang likes to cook with instant ramen. (As evidence, you can see the first issue of *Lucky Peach* or the videos of him doing so on our website.) One of his finest creations was an instant-ramen lasagna that took all of the skills and powers of one of his most talented lieutenants, Tony Kim, to conjure. (The instant ramen was powderized into flour, re-formed into dough sheets, cut, and baked.) We have extracted and unengineered the sauce that went inside it for your easy home enjoyment here.

Sichuanese Chopped Celery with Beef

**Makes 2 main-course servings with noodles
or 4 servings as part of a multidish meal with rice**

+	kosher salt
2 C	diced (½") celery
1 T	neutral oil
4 oz	ground beef
1½ T	doubanjiang or gochujang (spicy chili-bean paste)
1½ T	finely chopped fresh ginger
1 t	soy sauce
1 t	Chinkiang vinegar
+	cooked fresh wheat noodles (lo mein or ramen), rice noodles, spaghetti, or rice if that's what you feel like having

1 Bring a few cups of salted water to a boil in a saucepan. Blanch the celery for 30 seconds, then drain and rinse in a colander under cold water.

2 Heat a wok or cast iron skillet over high heat and coat with the oil. When the oil is shimmering, add the ground beef and stir-fry until cooked through, using a spoon to break the meat into small pieces. Add the chili-bean paste and continue to stir until the fat in the pan has taken on the color of the chili paste. Add the ginger and stir-fry until fragrant, just a few seconds more, then add the celery.

3 Continue to stir-fry until the celery is hot and coated with sauce. Finish with the soy sauce and vinegar. At this point the sauce may be refrigerated or frozen. Reheat before proceeding. Serve over noodles or rice.

When we were making the "All You Can Eat" issue of _Lucky Peach,_ we got to thinking about celery a lot, because, you know, after you pick a stalk or two out of a celery heart for tuna salad or stock, what do you do with the rest? How does one eat through the celery without resorting to some cheap trick like ants on a log? One solution came from Gabrielle Hamilton of New York City's Prune: She braised celery stalks in meat sauce, then served the tender vegetables topped with the same rich ragu.

Now, how to make it "Asian"? Fuchsia Dunlop provided the answer. Fuchsia is the foremost English-language authority on Chinese cooking, someone who has educated scores of Westerners (_Lucky Peach_ included!) on the flavor strategies of Sichuan cooking. Her book _Every Grain of Rice_ was a real departure for her—it was about making Chinese food accessible to readers who might be anxious about cooking it at home. This recipe from the book, which came out during my extended phase of celery meditation, has stuck with me—I'm happy to adapt it here. It's not really a ragu, more of a stir-fry, but since its backstory comes from ragu, and since quotation marks give you license to do whatever you want, we're including it here in the "ragu" section. I'll also note that while we've suggested these recipes as sauces for noodles, both this and the Sichuan Pork Ragu (page 136) are excellent over rice.

Rices

Fried Rice, Two Ways

Makes 2 main-course or 4 side-dish servings

3 C	cooked and cooled long-grain rice (preferably a day old)
+	STUFF (pages 144 and 145)
+	SAUCE (pages 144 and 145)
2 T	neutral oil
2	large eggs, beaten
1 T	chopped garlic
1 T	chopped fresh ginger
2	scallions, thinly sliced, whites and greens separated
+	FLOURISHES (page 145, optional)

1 Put the rice in a large bowl and break up any clumps with your hands. Set the rice, the **STUFF**, and the **SAUCE** in 3 separate bowls near the stove.

2 Heat 1 tablespoon of the oil in a wok or heavy skillet over high heat. Pour the eggs into the skillet and cook, folding the cooked egg up and over itself until set but still glossy and tender, about 30 seconds. Remove to a plate and return the pan to the heat.

3 Add the remaining 1 tablespoon oil to the pan, then, a moment later, the garlic, ginger, and scallion whites. Stir-fry for just a few seconds, then add the **STUFF.** Continue stir-frying until hot and cooked through, 1 to 3 minutes.

4 Dump the rice into the pan and toss to mix. Use a spatula to spread the rice out and maximize contact with the hot pan. Stir and fold once a minute for 3 minutes, until all of the rice is hot and a little charred in spots.

5 Pour the **SAUCE** over the rice and toss to coat everything. This is a good moment to consider investing in a wok spatula for next time. Honestly, I'm surprised you've made it this far without one. You're worth it!

6 Keep cooking, tossing, spreading, and tossing again, until the rice is evenly colored and looks pleasantly dry. Return the scrambled eggs to the pan, chopping a couple of times to break them up, and toss in the scallion greens and any last-minute **FLOURISHES.** Eat.

This recipe takes one technique for frying rice and shows two paths it can travel based simply on the STUFF and the SAUCE that you pour in. The variations are endless. Also, if you happen to be ordering takeout, throw an extra rice on your order, and you're teed up perfectly to make fried rice the following day.

Chinese Sausage Fried Rice

Stuff

½ C   thin coins of Chinese sausage (preferable) or diced bacon or pancetta (if you can't be with the one you love, love the one you're with)

½ C   frozen peas

Sauce (whisked together)

1 T   Shaoxing wine or dry sherry

1 T   fish sauce or soy sauce

1 t   sugar

½ t   sesame oil

Fried Rice Made Nice

We advise portioning out all your ingredients in advance like you're a host on Cooking Channel. Sauce in one bowl, stuff in another, minced prep in another still. This is how it's done in pro kitchens and streetside stalls, and the reason is that it works!

Thai Herb Fried Rice

Stuff
½	large shallot, minced
4 oz	ground pork

Sauce (whisked together)
1 T	fish sauce, or more to taste
1 t	sugar
10	grinds white pepper (scant ⅛ t)

Flourishes
½ C	herbs (picked mint leaves, torn basil leaves, cilantro stems and leaves)
+	lime wedges (for serving, not tossing in the rice)

Taking the egg out of the pan and adding it back in ensures that it will stay fluffy and yellow and tender. We could be accused of being fussy here. It would be easier to let the eggs get all Hammer-timed—overcooked to squeaky, sulfury shreds. It's up to you whether or not to treat your eggs like parachute pants in the nineties, but we think this method is easy and nice.

Herbs is good, man. If you have cilantro hanging out and no plans for it, put it on top of your fried rice. Same for any fresh herb that makes sense with the flavors you're using—put down the rosemary. A high pile of herbs on a bowl of fried rice makes it seem fancy for some reason, and it eats well.

Ume Rice

Makes 2 side-dish servings

1–2	umeboshi
2	shiso leaves
2 C	freshly cooked short-grain rice

Pit and mince the plums to yield 1 tablespoon. Thinly slice the shiso leaves, discarding their stems. Gently fold the minced plum and shiso into the rice.

Kabocha Rice

Makes 4 to 6 side-dish servings

1½ C	rice (preferably short-grain)
1 C	diced (¼") kabocha squash
1 T	sake
½ t	kosher salt
1½ C	water

1 Rinse the rice in a few changes of cold water until the water runs clear. Drain well.

2 Combine the rice, kabocha squash, sake, salt, and water in a rice cooker or heavy-lidded pot. Cook according to rice cooker directions until the rice is tender and the squash is cooked (or set the pot over medium heat for 5 minutes, then turn to low and simmer until the rice is tender and the liquid is absorbed, about 20 minutes).

Variety is the spice of rice. Don't get stuck in a rut. Jazz it up. Take a risk. Get creative. Think of the possibilities: You could use mint instead of shiso, sweet potato instead of kabocha. It's your rice, after all.

Ume Rice

Jumuk Bap

Beef

3 oz	lean ground beef
1 T	soy sauce
1 T	grated fresh pear or pear juice, apple cider, or pineapple juice
1 t	sugar
¼ t	minced garlic
¼ t	sesame oil
+	freshly ground black pepper

Bap

1½ C	cooked short-grain rice (do not rinse or wash the rice before cooking it)
2 t	sesame oil
1	sheet nori, torn into small bits

1 Prepare the beef: Mix together the beef, soy sauce, pear, sugar, garlic, sesame oil, and a pinch of pepper. Cover with plastic wrap and marinate at room temperature for 15 minutes or in the fridge for up to 1 hour.

2 Heat a small skillet over medium heat and add the beef and marinade. Cook, stirring to break up the meat, until the meat is browned and cooked through and the pan looks dry, 3 to 5 minutes. Remove from the heat and set aside.

3 Make the bap: Put the rice into a large bowl and drizzle with the sesame oil. Briefly mix together with your hands (you may want to wear disposable plastic gloves). Add the cooked ground beef and nori and mix again. Roll the mixture into 1-inch balls (about 2 tablespoons each), compacting gently so the rice sticks together. Serve warm or refrigerate for later snacking.

The idea behind jumuk bap is almost laughably simple: Mix some meat with some rice and squish it into a ball. That's it. I thought it might be a good way to repurpose leftovers from a Korean feast at home, but the dish gradually took on a life of its own around the house. The jumuk bap are fun to eat for little children and old men alike, and once chilled, they're sturdy enough to pack up in your kids' lunch boxes!

Onigiri

Makes 6 onigiri

4 C	freshly cooked short-grain rice (still hot)
+	sea salt
+	filling (choose one): umeboshi, mayonnaisey tuna salad, chopped parsley (see below for amounts)
+	one of the following (optional): sesame seeds, 8" x 2" strips toasted nori

1 Set up your onigiri-building station: Arrange a rice cooker or pot with cooked rice, bowls with salt and filling, and a dish of water within arm's reach. Have ready a plate or baking sheet on which you will place your formed onigiri. If using sesame seeds, scatter on a plate.

2 Fluff the rice with a fork. (For parsley onigiri, add 2 tablespoons chopped parsley and a little salt.) Wet your hands in the dish of water and sprinkle them with salt. Scoop about ⅔ cup rice into your hand and make a 1-inch hollow in the center of the rice with your finger. Then:

For umeboshi: Place 1 plum into the hollow, then seal the rice over the filling. Roll the rice into a ball, then gently shape and compact it with your salted hands, gradually forming a 1-inch-thick triangular shape.

For tuna: Place 1 tablespoon tuna salad into the hollow, then seal the rice over the filling. Roll the rice into a ball, then gently shape and compact it with your salted hands, gradually forming a 1-inch-thick triangular shape.

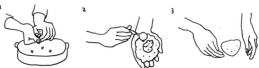

For parsley: Gently shape and compact the parsley-flecked rice with your salted hands, gradually forming a 1-inch-thick triangular shape.

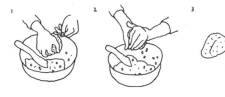

3 If desired, wrap each onigiri with a strip of toasted nori or roll in sesame seeds to coat.

Variation: Turn these into yaki onigiri. Heat a cast iron skillet over medium heat. Add the onigiri to the pan and cook until a light crust forms, about 2 minutes. Flip and brush lightly with soy sauce. Cook until a crust forms on the other side. Flip and brush with soy sauce. Cook until golden brown and crisp, flipping as necessary, until crisp all over, about 5 minutes.

An anytime snack, ideal for picnics, popular with children. The salted-hand technique outlined here comes from my friend Miki Tanaka, and is the secret to killer onigiri.

Kimbap
(page 154)

Kimbap

Makes 4 servings

4 C	freshly cooked short- or medium-grain rice
1 t	sesame oil, plus more as needed
½ t	rice vinegar
+	kosher salt
4	sheets nori

+3 or 4 of the following, cut into matchsticks

~½ C	carrots
~½ C	cucumber
~½ C	pickled daikon
½–1 C	ham, imitation crab, or any appealing leftover meat
1	egg crepe/omelet (cook 2 beaten large eggs in a large skillet without stirring until set in a thin sheet)

1 Mix the rice, sesame oil, vinegar, and a sprinkle of salt in a medium bowl. Lightly toast a sheet of nori by waving it seven or eight times a few inches above a gas burner. Lay the nori on a sushi mat and spread 1 cup of the seasoned rice across the end closest to you (the rice should cover one-third of the nori with the empty space farthest from you).

2 Arrange one-quarter of the fillings ½ inch in from the edge of the rice closest to you in an even pile that runs the width of your nori. Pick up the edge of the mat closest to you and roll away from your body, pressing down evenly across the log as you go, encasing the filling in a snug sleeping bag of rice and nori. Repeat for the remaining nori, rice, and fillings. Moisten a paper towel with a bit of sesame oil and use it to wipe the blade of a sharp knife before slicing.

Kimbap are an unfussy and more robust cousin of Japanese sushi rolls. Dave Chang brought them on a train ride we took to Washington, D.C., and since then they've always been "train food" to me, though they are equally good on road trips, plane trips, and picnics.

Sticky Rice Wrapped in Lotus Leaves

Makes 4 servings

4	dried shiitake mushrooms
2	large dried lotus leaves
1½ C	sticky (sometimes called glutinous) rice
1½ C	cold water
1 T	neutral oil
2	Chinese sausages, sliced into thin coins
+	kosher salt and white pepper
½ C	minced shallots
3	garlic cloves, minced
4	scallions, chopped
1 T	Shaoxing wine
1 T	light brown sugar
2 T	soy sauce
1 T	oyster sauce
1 T	chopped fresh ginger

1 Soak the shiitakes in hot water for 30 minutes. Drain and roughly chop.

2 Cut the lotus leaves in half, put them in a large bowl or a plugged sink, and cover them in hot water. Let them soak while you cook the rice and filling.

3 Combine the rice and cold water in a medium saucepan. Bring to a boil over high heat. Reduce the heat to a simmer, cover, and set a timer for 15 minutes. Scoop the rice into a wide bowl and let it cool for a few minutes.

4 Meanwhile, heat the oil in a wok over medium–high heat until shimmering. Add the sausages and brown for 1 minute. Toss in the shiitakes, season with salt and white pepper, and stir–fry until they have dried out slightly and are turning brown around the edges, about 3 minutes. Add the shallots, garlic, and half of the scallions. Cook for 30 seconds, keeping everything moving so you don't burn the garlic. Reduce the heat slightly and stir in 2 tablespoons water, the wine, sugar, soy sauce, and oyster sauce. Cook for 1 to 2 minutes, then remove the wok from the heat, fold in the ginger and remaining scallions, and set aside.

5 Once the rice is cooled, scoop the sausage mixture over the rice and gently fold to combine.

6 Remove the lotus leaves from their soaking bowl, pat them dry, and trim off the tough center stem. Lay half a leaf on your work surface with the cut side closest

(recipe continues)

to you. Place one-quarter of the rice filling in the center of the leaf and coax it into a rectangular mass. Fold the cut side (bottom edge) of the leaf up and over the pile of rice. Then fold in the left side of the leaf followed by the right side. Tightly roll and tuck until you're left with a neat little packet the size of an index card. Repeat with the remaining leaves and filling. Tie the finished packets snugly with kitchen twine.

7 Set up a steamer over high heat. When it reaches full steam, nestle the packets into the steamer and cook for 15 minutes. Serve hot, or cool to room temperature and refrigerate. The wrapped rice packets will keep for up to 2 days in the fridge. Reheat in a steamer or the microwave.

You've had *lap mei fan*—the steamed lotus-wrapped packages of soy-saucy sticky rice studded with Chinese sausage and other meats—at dim sum. Now you can have them at home! (Or *ma*.) You could substitute all manner of foliage for the difficult-to-source lotus leaves, which are inedible and inelegant to work with on account of their brittleness and size, but there's something about the specific flavor they impart that makes them essential to this dish.

Omurice

Makes 1 serving

1 T	butter
1	skinless, boneless chicken thigh (about 4 oz), cut into 1" pieces
¼ C	minced onion
1 C	cooked rice (preferably a day old)
+	kosher salt and freshly ground black pepper
2 T	ketchup, plus more for serving
2 T	frozen green peas
1	large egg, beaten
+	neutral oil

1 Melt the butter in a large skillet over medium heat. Add the chicken and cook until opaque but not quite cooked through, about 2 minutes. Add the onion and cook, stirring frequently, until the chicken is cooked through and the onion is translucent, 4 to 5 minutes longer.

2 Add the rice and cook, tossing and folding to combine and heat through, about 2 minutes. Season with salt and pepper.

3 Push the rice to the edges of the pan, clearing a 3-inch landing zone in the bottom of the pan. Add the ketchup to the bare spot in the pan and stir with a silicone spatula for 30 seconds until lightly caramelized. Mix the rice and ketchup until combined, about 1 minute. Add the frozen peas and toss to heat through. Transfer the rice mixture to a bowl and keep warm.

4 Season the egg with a pinch of salt. Heat a couple of drops of oil in an 8-inch nonstick skillet. Pour the egg mixture into the pan, swirling to coat the pan in a thin, even layer. Let the egg crepe cook until the top is set, then spoon the fried rice onto one half of the crepe. Fold the egg over the rice and slide the omelet onto a plate. Serve with ketchup.

Most cooks and chefs say that the simplicity or the cleanliness or the precision of Japanese cuisine is the beacon that drew them to it. For me it was learning that the Japanese believe it is 100 percent okay to absolutely house your eggs in ketchup. Omurice (aka rice-filled omelets) are a fixture of college students' diets and of lonely salarymen who hang out in *kissaten*, the Westernized coffee shops that are a relic of Japan's post–WWII reconstruction era. This ain't fancy *kaiseki* food, but if you're a ketchup-and-eggs person, it's mighty fine eating.

Warm
Vegetables

Eat Your Greens

Serve these communally with anything and everything in this book.

Greens with Whole Garlic
(page 164)

Bok Choy with Oyster Sauce
(page 165)

Dry-Fried Green Beans
(page 164)

Greens with Whole Garlic

Makes 4 servings

2 T	neutral oil	**1 lb**	pea greens or large spinach (i.e., not baby) or bok choy (babies halved lengthwise or big guys sliced)
6	garlic cloves, peeled but whole	**¼ C**	chicken broth

1 Pour the oil into a wok and add the garlic cloves. Set the wok over medium heat and warm the oil so the garlic sizzles. Turn the cloves, caramelizing them evenly, for 2 to 3 minutes. (Note that if you're not cooking in a wok, maybe you wanna cock the pan up sideways so the oil pools around the garlic cloves during this stage, to imitate wok-ish proportions. There's a subtle difference to cooking something in even a minor depth of oil—as there would be in the wok—in that the oil is going to get less hammered during the browning process and pick up more and better garlic flavor.)

2 Add the greens and toss to coat in the oil. Add the broth and cover the skillet, cooking the greens until wilted and just tender, about 2 minutes. Serve the greens with the garlic cloves.

Dry-Fried Green Beans

Makes 4 servings

2 T	neutral oil	**¼ C**	chopped scallions
1 lb	green beans, whole, or Chinese long beans, cut into 4" lengths	**½ t**	sambal oelek or *Sambal* (page 254)
1 T	chopped garlic	**1 T**	soy sauce
1 T	chopped fresh ginger	**½ t**	sugar
		+	kosher salt

1 Heat 1 tablespoon of the oil in a wok over medium heat. After a minute (or as soon as the oil is getting to the *oh shit this oil means business* level of heat), add the green beans and stir-fry until they start to shrivel and turn brown, 8 minutes. Transfer to a plate.

2 Turn the heat up to high and add the remaining 1 tablespoon oil. Add the garlic, ginger, and scallions. Stir-fry for a few seconds until fragrant, then add the sambal. Add the green beans, soy sauce, and sugar. Toss until the beans are coated in sauce and heated through. Season to taste with salt and serve immediately.

Bok Choy with Oyster Sauce

Makes 4 servings

+	kosher salt
+	neutral oil
2 T	chopped garlic
1 lb	baby bok choy
2 T	oyster sauce, or more to taste

1 Bring a large pot of salted water to a boil.

2 Meanwhile, heat ½ inch oil in a small pot over medium heat. Add the garlic and gently cook until the garlic is golden brown. Remove with a slotted spoon and drain on a plate lined with paper towels. Set the pan with the garlic oil aside.

3 Add the bok choy to the boiling water and blanch until crisp-tender, about 2 minutes. The leaves will go limp; the heart of the bok choy should offer only a little resistance to the tip of a knife. Drain well and blot with paper towels to remove excess water.

4 Arrange the bok choy on a platter and drizzle with the oyster sauce. Drizzle with a little of the reserved garlic oil and sprinkle with the fried garlic.

IMPORTANT: Taste your oyster sauce! Some are saltier or more concentrated than others, and may need to be thinned out with a few spoonfuls of water or broth.

Miso-Glazed Eggplant

Makes 4 to 6 servings

4	Japanese eggplants, halved lengthwise
1 T	neutral oil
¼ C	red miso
2 T	mirin
+	sesame seeds

1 Heat the oven to 450°F. (Lazy power move: Line a baking sheet with parchment paper to make cleanup supereasy.)

2 Slick the eggplants all over with oil and arrange them cut-side up on the baking sheet. Roast for 10 minutes—they should be barely wilted, a very light roast.

3 Meanwhile, whisk together the miso and mirin in a small bowl.

4 Smear the cut side of the eggplants with the miso mixture and roast until the eggplants are tender and the miso is browned and bubbling, 10 minutes longer. Sprinkle with sesame seeds and serve.

This is one of those center-of-the-plate types of vegetable preparations that can easily supplant meat. (Serve it with short-grain rice and any of the pickles in this book, or with store-bought kimchi.) The eggplants take on a super-rich caramelly umami flavor. It's a standard Japanese response to the part of the summer when there's more eggplant around than anyone knows what to do with, and it works very well on a grill—just put the eggplants over a low-to-medium fire, so the miso doesn't burn too fast and the flesh of the eggplant has time to cook all the way through.

Roasted Squash with Red Glaze

Makes 6 to 8 servings

2 lbs	mixed hard squash (such as delicata, kabocha, and acorn), seeded and cut into 1" wedges
2 T	neutral oil
+	kosher salt and freshly ground black pepper
1 T	minced fresh ginger
1 T	minced garlic
¼ C	minced scallions, plus more for garnish
2 T	water
¼ C	soy sauce
2 T	mirin
1 T	rice vinegar
1 T	sugar

1 Heat the oven to 400°F. Line a baking sheet with parchment paper.

2 Toss the squash with 1 tablespoon of the oil, season with salt and pepper, and arrange on the baking sheet. Roast until tender, about 35 minutes.

3 Meanwhile, heat the remaining 1 tablespoon oil in a medium saucepan over medium heat. Add the ginger, garlic, and scallions and sweat until soft and fragrant, about 2 minutes. Stir in the water, soy sauce, mirin, vinegar, and sugar. Bring to a simmer and cook until the glaze is syrupy, about 8 minutes.

4 Drizzle the roasted squash with the glaze and sprinkle with more scallions. (The squash in the photo have not had their second dose of scallions yet.) Serve.

This kind of red glaze is traditionally put over all kinds of meat: We figured why not try it on a center-of-the-plate vegetable like squash? The result is a savory-sweet and compulsively eatable vegetable you can build a meal around.

Stir-Fried Asparagus

Makes 4 servings

+	kosher salt
1	large bunch asparagus (can also sub green beans or broccoli rabe), cut into 2" pieces
2 T	neutral oil
2 T	chopped garlic
1 t	sambal oelek or a couple small fresh chilies, finely chopped
2 T	fish sauce
¼ C	oyster sauce
1 T	sugar
+	white pepper
½ C	chicken stock

1 Bring a large pot of water to a boil and salt it well. Blanch the asparagus for a minute or two.

2 Meanwhile, heat the oil in a wok over medium heat. Add the garlic and cook until fragrant but not browned.

3 Drain the asparagus in a colander, shake them dry for a few seconds (a little water is not a problem), and toss into the wok. Crank the heat all the way up.

Stir-fry for a minute. Add the sambal and fish sauce and stir-fry for a few seconds. Add the oyster sauce, sugar, and a few grinds of white pepper. Stir-fry for a few more seconds, then add the stock and cook until the sauce is thicker than water but nowhere near a glaze, just a couple minutes.

4 Serve on a large platter or in a shallow bowl. Eat hot.

This is a recipe copped from Andy Ricker of the Pok Pok restaurant empire, who has written a book on Thai cooking that is essential English-language reading for anybody who wants to go down the rabbit hole of effort and authenticity to produce truly great Thai cooking at home.

Otherwise, this preparation, which Andy shared with me as a way of cooking fiddlehead ferns, has become an oft-used approach to Thai-style veg cookery in my house, particularly in the spring, when fiddleheads and asparagus are in season.

Warm Eggplant with Green Peppers

Makes 6 to 8 servings

1½ lbs	small eggplants (preferably Japanese)
¼ C	neutral oil
6	garlic cloves
3	long green chili peppers or Italian frying peppers, cut into 1" pieces
+	kosher salt

1 Bring a large pot of water to a boil. Add the eggplants and cook until completely tender but not falling apart, about 20 minutes. Remove with tongs to a plate or baking sheet lined with paper towels. Set aside to cool.

2 Meanwhile, heat the oil in a large skillet over low heat. Add the garlic and cook, turning with tongs, until all sides are lightly golden and the garlic is tender, about 6 minutes. With a slotted spoon, transfer the garlic to a bowl or large mortar.

3 Increase the heat under the skillet to medium, add the peppers, and cook, turning, so all sides blister and brown. Do not let the oil smoke or turn dark.

4 Remove the stems from the eggplants and cut lengthwise into quarters. (If they are very long, cut crosswise to yield 3 × 1-inch hunks of eggplant.) Add to the bowl with the garlic.

5 With a slotted spoon, scoop the peppers into the bowl with the eggplant and garlic. Season with salt and pour in a little drizzle of the garlic-pepper oil. Begin mashing with a spoon or pestle. Add more oil and keep mashing to yield a rich but not too oily mixture. The amount of oil you use will depend on the innate texture of the flesh of your eggplant. Re-season with salt to taste and serve warm.

During the conceptualization phase of this book, we'd eat lunch around town in different restaurants, meeting about this or that issue, hammering out a schedule. This was a dish we ordered on a whim from a place called the Bao, which, at the moment I am typing this, serves the best *xiao long bao* in New York. I can't believe that is true, since it's on a touristy stretch of St. Mark's Place, instead of hidden in a mall in Flushing, but the truth is the truth. Anyway, our Italian photographer immediately said this dish could be Italian, and it could. It could be from anywhere eggplants and peppers grow and go together, and it's served in a weird little wooden mortar and pestle, for mushing the tender and oily fruits together. (They'd probably be a little more wilted and cooked than they are in this picture, honestly!) Serve it as a side with a Chinese or Italian meal. Nobody's gonna mind.

Corn Cheese

Makes 6 to 8 servings

4 oz	bacon, chopped (about ¾ C)
2 T	butter
1 lb	frozen corn kernels (about 3 C) or the kernels cut from 3–4 ears fresh corn
4 oz	cream cheese
1 T	white miso
2 T	mayonnaise
1 C	shredded mozzarella cheese

1 Heat the oven to 450°F.

2 Place the bacon in a large, cold skillet and set over medium heat. Cook, stirring often, until the bacon is crispy and its fat rendered, about 10 minutes.

3 Pour off most of the fat from the pan and toss in the butter. When the butter melts and sizzles, add the corn and toss to coat. Cook for 2 to 3 minutes to heat the corn through. Add the cream cheese and miso and use the back of a spoon to smush until they melt and coat the corn. Stir in the mayo and toss until the mixture is creamy and smooth.

4 Spoon the corn into a baking dish (or a fajita pan!) big enough to fit the corn mixture in a ½- to 1-inch layer. Sprinkle with the mozzarella and bake until browned and bubbling, 5 to 7 minutes.

Corn cheese is a Korean drinking snack, one that I have never eaten a version of that I would describe as "good." Still, I order it, we all order it, with our grapefruit *makkoli* and our huge bottles of Hite and all that inadvisable *soju*. And sure as the clear liquid drains from the glass, the corn disappears from the table. There's something about corn cheese that's hard to say no to.

Since I think a "traditional" corn cheese would be disappointing and gross to anyone not accustomed to it/not already drunk, we've turbocharged ours. Now there's bacon, which makes all food better, and cream cheese in place of most of the mayonnaise that's sometimes used to sauce up the corn, because cream cheese is as delicious an emulsifier as exists. Note that the mozzarella called for here should not have been lovingly wrung from a Southern Italian buffalo, but instead whatever your supermarket stocks, possibly pre-shredded.

Roasted Sweet Potatoes

Makes as many servings as you'd like

+   sweet potatoes

Heat the oven to 400°F. Line a baking sheet with parchment paper. Arrange the sweet potatoes on the baking sheet and roast until they are very tender and their aroma fills the room, about 45 minutes to 1 hour. A few spots will leak bubbling caramel. The timing will depend on the size, density, age, and variety of the potato, but don't undercook them. They are somewhat forgiving if you forget them, but don't let them go so long that they dry out or burn. Wrap in foil (so you can hold them) and eat hot.

I know that it's not exactly a mind-blowing recipe to say "Hey, go bake a potato," but the baked sweet potato is an unheralded snack food. When we decided we wanted to put one in the book, the team sent out feelers to find the Asian loaded baked potato—something with a trashy *Lucky Peach* zing to it.

But it doesn't exist, or not widely. Then one night, after days of cooking and photographing and eating soy-saucy this and chili-spiked that, we finished the day with these potatoes. And we all ended up getting behind the sentiment: Sometimes a baked sweet potato is all you need.

I first heard about them, about this way of eating sweet potatoes, from my friend Miki Tanaka, who told me stories of snow-blanketed winter in her seaside Japanese town, where, down quiet streets, she would come upon a beacon of warmth and light: a vendor selling hot, foil-wrapped potatoes cooked over a wood fire. They were the seasonal food that signaled the arrival of short days and long, starry nights.

Writer Naomi Duguid praised baked potatoes in China in our Street Food issue, and editor Joanna Sciarrino corroborates her account. "There's no shortage of interesting and delicious street food in the back alleys of Shanghai—steamy *baozi* buns, slippery *liangpi* noodles, overstuffed *jian bing* crepes," she told me, recalling her days as student there. "Nothing was a better snack than the nearly saccharine coal-roasted sweet potatoes [*kao di gua*] sold out of enormous iron drums for a couple of yuan [about 50 cents]. I liked them mostly because they tasted good, but also because I liked the idea of eating a potato on the go."

We offer the suggestion of snacking on baked sweet potatoes not to cheat you out of a more complicated recipe, but because sometimes you don't need one.

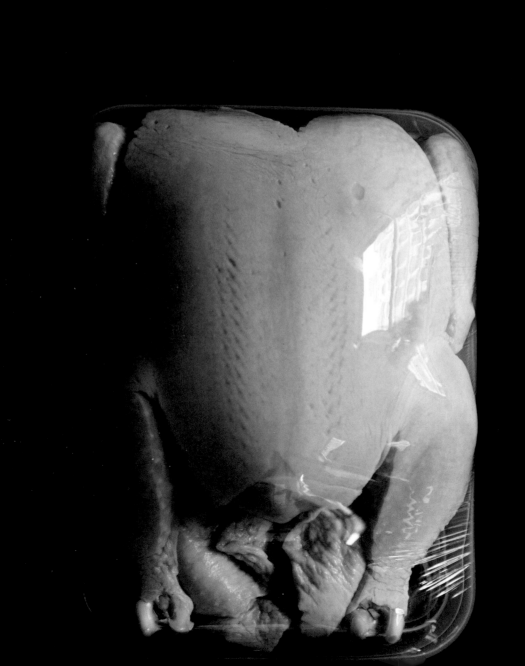

Chicken

Chinese Roast Chicken

We do not trade lightly in imperatives at *Lucky Peach*, but this one is easy: You should be roasting chickens at home.

Aside from their fundamental deliciousness and incomparable versatility, they are also The Gift That Keeps on Giving.

At my house we take the carcass and picked-over bones from a chicken dinner and throw them in a soup pot and cover them with water. By the time the kids are asleep, there are a couple quarts of a nice light chicken broth that crushes whatever they're turning out over at the old College Inn. That broth could be a soup the next day, a braising medium, something to cook rice in—and requires no special effort to make.

Because I love and respect you, I imagine you already know these things. Perhaps you already have a regular roast routine. Which is why we present you with these three Chinese-influenced options. They're just barely more work than the basic, unadorned, vaguely European birds most of the staff of *Lucky Peach* roasts up on the regular, so we hope these add much needed variety and spice to your lives, as they have done for ours.

We are advocates of a hot-and-lazy approach: one high temperature, one pan, one position, one great result. Furthermore:

CHILL IT OUT

Season the bird ahead of time and let it sit uncovered in the fridge overnight. (Kosher chickens are salted before you buy them, so don't salt those, just let 'em mellow in the fridge overnight.) That's not textbook-easy, not like "Thirty minutes after you leave the supermarket you'll have dinner on the table!" easy, but it's not hard either. I started doing this after I fell under the spell of Judy Rodgers's *Zuni Cafe Cookbook*. I view processing the chicken as such as part of my grocery shopping: The milk needs to go in the door of the fridge, the Cheerios go up in the snack cabinet, the chicken gets seasoned and put on a sheet pan so that it can be cooked sometime in the next one to three days. (Some of our favorite fancy restaurants age birds like this for five and more days, allowing surface moisture to evaporate to ensure a crisp skin.) To be très unscientific about it, the salting of the bird helps cure it, so you don't have to worry that it's going bad, waiting to be cooked.

Can you rush the birds from store to seasoning to oven to table? Of course. And they will be good. But a little bit of planning ups the finesse of the finished product a lot.

TRUSSY = TOO FUSSY

We're on the wrong side of history on this one. My argument is this: Roasting your bird with legs all akimbo means more skin is exposed to more direct heat, which means more deliciously burnished flesh. I like that. Plus there's no need to worry about when it's all done: When the legs are ready, you know the breast meat is too. With trussed birds, we feel like the inner-thigh zone gets underattended. We're not that kind of lover.

Lacquered
Roast Chicken
(page 183)

REST REQUIRED

You must budget in time for your bird to rest after it comes out of the oven. It makes the meat better for lots of reasons you don't need to fully grasp. Just know that this isn't a wives' tale; this is the truth. That fifteen minutes makes for better, juicier chicken.

BETTER BIRDS ARE WORTH IT

You don't need to buy some animal with a *Portlandia* backstory, but spending a few extra bucks to get a bird that wasn't reared in the death camps of a company like Perdue pays dividends at the table. There's a lot of confusing and unregulated agricultural nomenclature to sort through, but the term that really gets our hearts beating faster is "air-chilled"—poultry that has been processed with a very minimal amount of extra water, essentially. We like this because we like crisp skin, yes, but also because chicken processing water is definitely the liquid that flows through the rivers in our nightmares, and we want as little to do with it as possible.

HOW DO I KNOW WHEN IT'S DONE?

You can/should check the temperature where the breast and thigh meet as well as the thickest part of the breast: 165°F is the magic number. If you don't have a thermometer, the skin should be mahogany and the legs should wiggle freely at their joints, like you could almost tear them off. You can snip the skin between the thigh and breast and if the liquid inside is clear, you should be good to go. These indicators work with normally proportioned chickens, not those that have been unnaturally re-proportioned by the will of man.

Five-Spice Chicken

1	whole chicken (3–4 lb)	**1 T**	kosher salt
2 t	five-spice powder	**1 T**	neutral oil

1 Place the chicken on a rack set inside a rimmed baking sheet. Mix the five-spice powder and salt together in a small bowl. Rub the seasoning all over the chicken and refrigerate, uncovered, for at least 12 hours and up to 2 days.

2 Heat the oven to 400°F.

3 Brush the bird with the oil, taking care not to rub off any seasoning on the skin. Roast for 50 minutes. Let rest for 15 minutes before carving.

Lacquered Roast Chicken

1	whole chicken (3–4 lb)	**2 T**	soy sauce
2 T	honey or maltose	**2 t**	kosher salt

1 Place the chicken on a rack set inside a rimmed baking sheet. Stir together the honey and soy sauce until the honey dissolves. Using a pastry brush, coat the chicken in a thin, even layer of the mixture. Let stand at room temperature for 15 minutes to let the skin dry slightly, then brush again with all of the remaining lacquer. Sprinkle with the salt and refrigerate, uncovered, for at least 12 hours and up to 2 days.

2 Heat the oven to 400°F.

3 Roast the chicken for 50 minutes. If the skin darkens too quickly, tent with foil and continue roasting. Let rest for 15 minutes before carving.

Spicy Roast Chicken

1½ t	Sichuan peppercorns	**2 T**	kosher salt
1½ t	black peppercorns	**2 T**	neutral oil
8	garlic cloves, peeled	**1**	whole chicken (3–4 lbs)

1 If you have a mortar and pestle, smash the peppercorns together until finely ground. Add the whole garlic and salt and pound into a smooth paste. Stir in the oil. Otherwise, buzz the peppercorns in a spice grinder. Finely chop the garlic, sprinkle with salt, and crush into a paste with the wide, flat side of your chef's knife or cleaver. Combine the peppercorns and garlic paste in a small bowl and stir in the oil.

2 Place the chicken on a rack set inside a rimmed baking sheet. Smear the spice paste all over the bird. Refrigerate, uncovered, for at least 12 hours and up to 1 day.

3 Heat the oven to 400°F.

4 Roast the chicken for 50 minutes. Let rest for 15 minutes before carving.

Oyakodon

Makes 1 serving

¼ C	water
¼ t	hondashi
2 t	sugar
2 t	mirin
2 t	sake
1½ T	soy sauce
½ C	thinly sliced onions
1	chicken thigh, cut into ¾" pieces
2	large eggs, lightly beaten
1	scallion, cut into 1" lengths
+	cooked rice, for serving

1 Combine the water, hondashi, sugar, mirin, sake, soy sauce, onion, and chicken in an 8-inch nonstick skillet. Set over medium heat and bring to a boil. Reduce the heat and simmer until the chicken is cooked through, about 5 minutes.

2 Pour the eggs over the bubbling mixture and sprinkle the scallions on top. Cover and cook gently until the mixture is set but still custardy, a minute or two. Remove from the heat and let sit a minute. Slide on top of a big bowl of rice.

Oyakodon is one of the great alliances of the egg and the place it came from, a fundamental Japanese comfort food dish. It can be made with very little—a dash of this, a sliver of meat, a couple eggs—but the end result is greater than the sum of its parts.

Adobo

Angela Dimayuga
Chef of Mission Chinese
Food New York

Adobo is a common preparation in the Philippines. It's meat cooked in vinegar and soy plus bay leaf, black peppercorns, salt, and a lot of garlic.

A lot of the time, you sear the meat—adobo is usually made with either pork or chicken—then you braise it out. (I prefer chicken because the chicken skin gets super melty in that second step.) You're just hammering it down. When the meat is falling-off-the-bone tender, I remove it, reduce down the liquid in the pan, and then spoon it over the chicken and some rice as a sauce.

Filipino soy sauce is less intense than Chinese dark soy or Japanese tamari. It functions as a coloring agent, makes the braise darker. There's a Filipino brand—Silver Swan—that comes in a foggy weird bottle that looks like it shouldn't have food in it. That's my go-to.

Of course with something as fundamental as adobo, there are a lot of variations. What I described is the basic one you'll find around Manila and in Pampanga, which is where my family is from. But I remember one my older brother found in an old Filipino cookbook that called for you to sear the pork or chicken, then add coconut milk and chili flakes. That one's great because those are just things that you have at your house and you're like, *Oh! I have these frozen chicken legs.* You deglaze with canned coconut milk—scraping the fond (the tasty stuff left in the pan after browning meat) and then add all your liquids and braise it. Then if you like heat in it you can add chilies to it. It's richer and a good variation to have in the mix.

Then there's a crazy, crazy one that's like a squid adobo. You take whole squid, take the goop out, cut the head into rings and then reserve the ink sac. This is a quick one because squid cooks really quickly. You get a hot pan, sear the squid, and then add your soy sauce, bay leaf, and black peppercorn—basically everything else but the vinegar—and you break the ink sacs in there and let it simmer for 3 minutes on high, then you add your vinegar. It's this really dark squid ink sauce. Oftentimes there will be some fresh chilies cut up and added at the end.

Chicken
Adobo
(page 188)

Chicken Adobo

Makes 4 servings

1	small can (about 5 oz) coconut milk or ½ C water
1 C	soy sauce (look for a Filipino brand called Silver Swan)
½ C	distilled white or cane vinegar
1 t	black peppercorns
3	bay leaves (preferably fresh)
4	garlic cloves, smashed
1–2	small dried red chilies (optional)
4	bone-in, skin-on chicken legs, drumstick and thigh separated
+	cooked white rice, for serving

1 Pour the coconut milk, soy sauce, and vinegar into a large, lidded skillet and toss in the peppercorns, bay leaves, garlic, and chilies (if using). Bring to a simmer over medium–high heat. Add the chicken pieces, snuggling them into a single layer; the sauce should come about three-quarters of the way up the pieces. (If it doesn't, add more water.)

2 Return the sauce to a simmer, then cover the pan and reduce the heat to maintain a gentle simmer. Cook the chicken until the meat is very tender, right before the stage where it falls off the bone (you still want to be able to pick them up without falling apart, but barely) and the skin is melty, 45 minutes to 1 hour.

3 Remove the chicken pieces and continue simmering the sauce, over medium–high heat, until it reduces by half and the sauce thickens a little/turns syrupy/coats a spoon, about 5 minutes. The flavor should be concentrated but not overpoweringly salty/sour.

4 At this point, you can eat the chicken adobo. Or you can place the legs on a foil-lined baking sheet and broil them on high for 5 or so minutes, until the sauce glazes the skin and becomes a little crusty. Or, you can store the sauce and chicken separately for up to 3 days. Reheat the chicken in a 400°F oven or under the broiler. However you serve the adobo, have plenty of warm white rice on hand to soak up the sauce.

Hainan Chicken Rice

Makes 4 to 6 servings

Chicken
1	whole chicken (4 lb)
12 C	water
+	salt and white pepper
4	scallions, chopped
1	piece (1") fresh ginger, halved and smashed
2	garlic cloves, smashed

Rice
2	shallots
4	garlic cloves
1	piece (1") fresh ginger
1	piece (2") lemongrass
2 C	jasmine rice
2	bay leaves (use pandan leaves if you can find them!)

Soup
2	garlic cloves, crushed
1	piece (1") fresh ginger, sliced
2 t	sugar, or more to taste
+	kosher salt and white pepper

Assembly
2 T	soy sauce
1 T	sesame oil
+	chopped scallions
+	chopped cilantro
+	cucumber slices
+	sambal oelek
+	**Ginger-Scallion Sauce** (either one from page 246)

1 Prepare the chicken: Trim off any visible fat around the cavities of the chicken and set aside.

2 Fill a large pot with the water, salt it lightly, and bring to a boil.

3 Meanwhile, rub the chicken inside and out with about 1 tablespoon salt and white pepper to taste. Stuff the scallions, ginger, and garlic into the cavity of the chicken. Use a toothpick to close the skin flaps and seal everything inside.

4 Once the pot of water is boiling aggressively, put the chicken in the pot, breast-side up. The chicken should be submerged. Cook for 10 minutes, then turn the heat off. Cover and let the chicken sit in the pot with the heat off for 45 minutes.

5 Set up a large bowl of ice and water. Remove the chicken (save the poaching liquid) and plunge it immediately into the ice water. Let the bird sit in there for 10 minutes, then remove and dry completely. It should feel like a rubber chicken. Don't skip this step.

6 Make the rice: Pound the shallots, garlic, and ginger together with a mortar and pestle. Give the lemongrass a few hard smacks with the broad side of a knife.

(recipe continues)

7 Heat the reserved chicken fat in a large pot over medium heat for a couple minutes to render the fat. Add the aromatic paste and lemongrass to the pot and cook, stirring, until everything is fragrant and browned on the edges. Add the rice and stir it around the pot to coat it in the chicken fat and aromatics, about 2 minutes. Add 2½ cups of the reserved poaching liquid (reserve the remaining) and the bay leaves to the pot and bring to a boil (or transfer to a rice cooker and cook according to the rice cooker's instructions). Cover, reduce the heat to low, and simmer the rice undisturbed for 20 minutes. Then turn off the heat and let the pot sit for 10 minutes.

8 Make the soup: Add the garlic, ginger, and sugar to the remaining poaching liquid and boil for 5 minutes. Season with salt, white pepper, and additional sugar to taste. Dilute with water if it's too salty. Strain. That's your soup.

9 Break down the cooked chicken into white and dark meat, slicing the breast and thighs.

10 To assemble: Rice goes on the plate first, then pieces of chicken. Drizzle the soy sauce and sesame oil over the chicken, so every piece gets a hit of soy and sesame, and sprinkle scallions and cilantro all over. Serve with cucumber slices, sambal, and ginger–scallion sauce.

11 Ladle the soup into individual serving bowls and stir in some scallions and cilantro before serving.

Hainan Chicken Rice is a dish you'll find in any Southeast Asian country where there are Chinese immigrants. The basic method is universal: Poach a chicken, then use the liquid to make rice. In Vietnam, it's called *com ga hai nam*; in Thailand, it's *khao man kai*; in Cambodia, it's *bai mon*. In Vietnam, you might add fish sauce and lime leaves; in Thailand, winter gourd; in Cambodia, fried garlic chips. The Malaysian method is to cook the rice with pandan leaves and lemongrass; it's served with a chili sauce that's sweet, sour, and fragrant with calamansi lime juice. (Here we call for jarred sambal oelek.)

We've called for bay leaves in the rice in the name of ease here, but if you can find them, pandan leaves are the real flavor. Pandan is a tropical plant with leaves that resemble giant grass blades, taste vaguely like vanilla, and are used to flavor *kaya* (coconut jam), Malaysia's most beloved breakfast spread. Pandan enhances the fragrance and sweetness of jasmine rice. (There's even science to back this up: Pandan leaves and jasmine rice contain an identical flavor compound, 2-acetyl-1-pyrroline, that gives both of them their characteristic sweet aromas.) And the lemongrass brings brightness to what might otherwise be a meal too oppressively rich with chicken fat.

Mall Chicken

Makes 4 to 6 servings

⅓ C	honey
¼ C	ketchup
3 T	soy sauce
2 T	apple cider vinegar or distilled white vinegar
2 T	brown sugar
1 T	minced garlic
2 lbs	boneless, skinless chicken thighs or breasts, or a mix, cut into 1" pieces
+	kosher salt
¼ C	cornstarch
1 T	oil
2 T	sesame seeds, for topping
+	cooked white rice, for serving (optional)

1 Heat the oven to 375°F.

2 Whisk the honey, ketchup, soy sauce, vinegar, sugar, and garlic in a bowl until smooth.

3 Place the chicken in another bowl, season with a little salt, and dust with the cornstarch, tossing to coat and shaking off the excess.

4 Heat the oil in a large skillet over high heat. Working in batches, sear the chicken, forming a light crust. Transfer the chicken to a baking dish.

5 Pour the sauce over the chicken and toss to coat. Bake until the chicken is cooked through and the sauce is bubbling and thick, about 20 minutes. Scatter with sesame seeds.

Sticky-sweet chicken: This is what "Asian" food is to so much of America, maybe with a couple broccoli florets and some rice (preferably fried) to go with it. I'm not much for this kind of dish, but to pretend that 90 percent of what people order at Chinese-Asian establishments isn't some variation on this would be to deny the truth. So in an inclusive act of recognition, here's our goopy take on this motherless dish—a mash-up of all your food-court chickens, be they sweet 'n' sour, sesame, or attributed to General Tso—with the deep fryer subtracted from the equation to increase the ease and dial back the grease.

Korean Grilled Chicken

Makes 4 servings

2 T	gochujang or sriracha		½ t	kosher salt
2 T	honey		4	bone-in, skin-on chicken legs
1 T	white miso		2	scallions, chopped, for garnish
¼ C	water		+	cooked rice, kimchi, **Scallion Salad**
2 T	apple cider vinegar			(page 48), and lettuce leaves, for
2 T	grapeseed oil, plus more as needed			serving

1 Whisk together the gochujang, honey, miso, water, vinegar, oil, and salt in a small bowl until smooth.

2 Place the chicken in a zip-top bag and pour the marinade over. Seal the bag and massage the marinade into the legs to make sure they are coated. Marinate in the refrigerator for at least 1 hour and up to 48 hours.

3 When ready to cook, heat the oven to 400°F or set up a grill for indirect cooking (in a charcoal grill, heap the coals on one side of the kettle so there's a hot zone and a cooler zone).

4 Remove the chicken from the marinade, scraping off excess to avoid burning. Pour the marinade into a bowl and set aside.

For roasting: Place the legs skin-side up on a rack set inside a roasting pan. Roast for 45 minutes, basting twice with some of the reserved marinade during the last 15 minutes of cooking.

For grilling: Oil the grate with a paper towel soaked in oil and set the legs skin-side down over the warmest part of the fire for 2 to 3 minutes, then flip and sear the reverse side. Move to a slightly cooler spot on the grill, cooking indirectly over the coals to avoid flare-ups, for about 30 minutes. Brush with some reserved marinade and cook, flipping often over the hot coals, until a crust forms and the chicken is cooked through, about 10 minutes longer. Let the chicken rest for a few minutes before serving.

5 Sprinkle with scallions. Serve the chicken with rice, kimchi, scallion salad, and lettuce leaves.

This recipe and the Lemongrass Chicken (page 196) take a classic set of core flavors (Korean here, Viet there) and use time and a plastic bag to infuse them into chicken legs, aka what should be everybody's favorite part of the bird. The results are irresistible.

Lemongrass Chicken

Makes 4 servings

3	garlic cloves, chopped
1	shallot, roughly chopped
1	small green chili, such as serrano or jalapeño, chopped
¼ C	chopped lemongrass, from the meaty parts of 2 stalks
2 T	fish sauce
2 T	neutral oil, plus more as needed
2 t	sugar
½ t	kosher salt
½ t	turmeric
4	bone-in, skin-on chicken legs
+	lime wedges
+	cooked rice, herbs, and **Nuoc Cham** (page 252) if you have it!

1 Blend the garlic, shallot, chili, lemongrass, fish sauce, oil, sugar, salt, and turmeric until smooth.

2 Place the chicken in a zip-top bag and pour the marinade over. Seal the bag and massage the marinade into the legs to make sure they are coated. Marinate in the fridge for at least 1 hour and up to 48 hours.

3 When ready to cook, heat the oven to 400°F or set up a grill for indirect cooking (in a charcoal grill, heap the coals on one side of the kettle so there's a hot zone and a cooler zone).

4 Remove the chicken from the marinade, scraping off excess to avoid burning. Pour the marinade into a bowl and set aside.

For roasting: Place the legs skin-side up on a rack set inside a roasting pan. Roast for 45 minutes, basting twice with some of the reserved marinade during the last 15 minutes of cooking.

For grilling: Wipe the grate with an oiled paper towel and set the legs skin-side down over the hottest part of the fire for 2 to 3 minutes to brown the skin. Flip and sear the reverse side. Move to a slightly cooler spot on the grill, cooking indirectly over the coals to avoid flare-ups, for about 30 minutes. Brush with some reserved marinade and cook, flipping often over the hot coals, until a crust forms and the chicken is cooked through, about 10 minutes longer. Let the chicken rest for a few minutes before serving.

5 Serve the chicken with lime wedges, rice, herbs, and nuoc cham.

Braised Chicken Wings

Makes 2 to 4 servings

1 lb	chicken wings, separated into drum and wingettes	**2**	whole star anise
1 t	kosher salt	**1**	cinnamon stick (3")
1½ t	Shaoxing wine or sherry	**½ t**	Sichuan peppercorns
1	piece (2") fresh ginger, thinly sliced	**1**	dried red chili (optional)
1½ t	vegetable oil	**½ C**	water
2	garlic cloves, sliced	**1½ T**	soy sauce
		1 t	sugar

1 Place the chicken wings in a large bowl and sprinkle with the salt, wine, and half the ginger slices. Let stand for 10 minutes while gathering the remaining ingredients.

2 Heat the oil in a medium skillet or wok over medium-high heat. After a minute, add the wings and sear until golden on all sides, about 5 minutes. With tongs, return the wings to the bowl.

3 Add the remaining ginger and garlic slices to the pan. Cook for a few seconds until aromatic. Add the star anise, cinnamon, peppercorns, and chili (if using) and toast until fragrant, about 20 seconds. Deglaze the pan with the water and soy sauce, using a spatula to scrape up any stuck-on bits from the bottom of the pan. Return the wings and any accumulated juices to the pan and add just enough water so the wings are three-quarters submerged in liquid.

4 Simmer the wings over medium heat, flipping a couple of times so they cook evenly, until they are tender, about 25 minutes. Stir the sugar into the sauce, increase the heat to high, and simmer until the sauce is reduced and syrupy. The wings can be braised 1 day ahead. Cover and refrigerate. Rewarm with a splash of water in a skillet.

5 Pile the wings on a platter, drizzle with their sauce, and serve.

These are loosely inspired by (and photo an homage to) my friend Lucas Peterson's mom's chicken wings. I only ate them once, from a hulking aluminum roasting pan that was soon after sealed up and brought to a potluck for Lucas's little brother's high school swim team. I think Regina Kwan Peterson's wings were a little less aggressively red-flavored than these, but she'd be okay with them.

Secret admission here between friends: When you have eaten all the wings, which I find almost too easy all by myself, there will be congealing opaque goop at the bottom of the vessel you serve them in. This goop can be profitably saved and deposited in a pot of rice if you go in for that sort of flavorful-repurposing-of-food-garbage type of business.

Miso Claypot Chicken (No Claypot)

Makes 4 servings

2 T	soy sauce	**8**	fresh shiitake mushroom caps, thinly sliced, or 4 dried shiitakes, soaked, stemmed, and thinly sliced
1 T	oyster sauce		
1 T	Shaoxing wine		
1 T	white or red miso	**1 C**	jasmine rice, rinsed and drained
½ t	kosher salt	**1 C**	chicken stock or water
½ t	sugar	**1**	slice (¼" thick) fresh ginger
½ t	sesame oil	**2**	scallions, cut into 1" pieces
+	white pepper		
4	boneless, skin-on chicken thighs, cut into 1" pieces		

1 In a large bowl, whisk together the soy sauce, oyster sauce, wine, miso, salt, sugar, sesame oil, and a few grinds of white pepper. Add the chicken and mushrooms and fold to coat.

2 Combine the rice, stock, and ginger in a rice cooker or a small Dutch oven.

For a rice cooker: Scrape the chicken mixture and all of the marinade on top of the rice. Scatter with scallions. Cover, start the rice cooker, and cook until the cycle is done. Open the lid and check the chicken for doneness. Depending on your model, the chicken may need a couple more minutes to cook through. If it does, set the rice cooker for another cycle, press start, and check again in 5 minutes.

For a Dutch oven: Place over medium heat and cook for 5 minutes, until just simmering. Reduce the heat to low and cook until all the liquid is absorbed and the chicken is cooked through, about 25 minutes. Fluff the rice, scraping up the crust from the bottom of the pot.

3 Scoop out and serve by the bowlful, or eat it straight out of the rice cooker.

A one-pot meal for the ages. The rice in the bottom of the rice cooker will go all dark and delicious like an Asian *socarrat* on you. If you've got a timer on your rice cooker, you could conceivably dump it all in there in the morning and come home to hot dinner right when you walk through the door!

Chinese Chicken Salad

Makes 4 servings

Ginger Dressing

¼ C	chopped fresh ginger
¼ C	rice vinegar
2 T	honey
2 T	sugar
1 T	sesame oil
1 T	soy sauce
¼ t	Chinese five-spice powder
+	white pepper

Salad

8 C	thinly sliced napa cabbage
2 C	thinly sliced red cabbage
2 C	pea shoots
1 C	chopped scallions
1 C	thinly sliced snow peas
2 C	shredded cooked chicken
½ C	cilantro leaves
1 C	drained canned mandarin oranges
½ C	crisp chow mein noodles
¼ C	toasted slivered almonds
2 T	toasted sesame seeds

1 Make the dressing: Combine the ginger, vinegar, honey, sugar, sesame oil, soy sauce, five-spice, and a few grinds of white pepper in a blender and process until smooth.

2 Make the salad: Toss the cabbages, shoots, scallions, snow peas, chicken, cilantro, and dressing together in a large bowl. Divide among plates and top with the oranges, noodles, almonds, and sesame seeds.

Much like the Mall Chicken (page 192), this is about as Asian as David Carradine. But if you were young in the 1990s and ever visited Wendy's or the Cheesecake Factory—or Spago for that matter—or watched Martin Yan on PBS, you encountered this bizarre sweet-sour hodgepodge of no particular tradition at all. For much of our staff, it's a sentimental favorite. We present our best take on it here; serve with marathon rewatchings of *Clarissa Explains It All, My So-Called Life,* or whatever other cultural effluvia accompanied the rise of this salad.

Red Roast Pork
(Char Siu)
(page 216)

Meats

Beef Satay

Makes 4 main-course or 8 appetizer servings

1 lb	flank steak (or use pork shoulder!)		**2 t**	palm, raw, or light brown sugar
1 T	coriander seeds		**1 t**	kosher salt
1 t	cumin seeds		**½ C**	coconut cream (scooped from the top
¼ t	white or black peppercorns			of a 15 oz can of coconut milk)
1	stalk lemongrass		**+**	neutral oil
1	piece (1") fresh ginger, sliced		**+**	**Peanut Sauce** (opposite), for
1	garlic clove, roughly chopped			serving
1 t	turmeric			

1 Slice the beef against the grain with a sharp knife set at a slight angle to the cutting board into pieces that are as long as the meat is wide (about 6 inches) and no more than ¼ inch thick, and 1½ to 2 inches wide. Place the meat in a nonreactive container or a large zip-top bag.

2 Toast the coriander, cumin, and peppercorns in a dry skillet over medium heat until you can smell the cumin, about 1 minute. Transfer the seeds to a large mortar and let cool for a couple of minutes.

3 Meanwhile, trim and discard the root end of the lemongrass, then chop the fattest 3 inches of the lemongrass stalk into thin coins.

4 Grind the toasted spices with a pestle. Add the lemongrass, ginger, and garlic and pound everything to a paste. Add the turmeric, sugar, and salt and pound some more. Stir in the coconut cream. Spoon the marinade over the beef and mix to coat. Cover or seal and refrigerate overnight.

5 Soak long wooden skewers in cold water for 30 minutes. Remove the meat from the marinade, wipe off any excess, then thread it onto the skewers.

6 Build a fire in a grill or heat a grill pan over medium heat—you want just enough heat to brown the meat effectively, but not so hot that the marinade will scorch. Oil the grate well. Cook the satay, turning occasionally, until browned and crusty, about 5 minutes. Serve with peanut sauce.

Have you ever had meat on a stick? Did you notice how much you enjoyed it and how much everyone around you enjoyed it and was enjoying themselves? That's because meat on a stick is one of the high-water marks of human invention, up there with the wheel and Ouija boards.

Notes on increasing the easiness of this dish: You can always process the marinade ingredients in a food processor or blender if your forearms are weak and you're afraid of the mortar and pestle. No one will judge you for using electricity and living on the grid when a simple primitive tool would do a better job and not drain our natural resources.

Peanut Sauce

Makes a scant ½ cup

The satay has nose-filling aromatics; this simple peanut sauce anchors the spices with deep and salty peanutiness.

¼ C	creamy peanut butter
2 T	hot water* (plus more if needed)
1 T	soy sauce
½ t	minced garlic

Stir everything together until fully incorporated. Add more water by the teaspoonful to thin the sauce, if needed. A squeeze of lime might be nice! Taste and see the goodness of the sauce.

*Or you could replace the water with coconut milk from the can you stole the cream from for the satay!

Cumin Lamb

Makes 2 to 4 servings

2 T	cumin seeds
1 T	Sichuan peppercorns
1 t	kosher salt
½–1 t	chili flakes
1 lb	boneless lamb leg, thinly sliced
2 T	neutral oil
2 C	thinly sliced white or yellow onions
1 C	sliced scallion, whites and greens
1 T	sliced garlic
2 T	soy sauce
2 T	Shaoxing wine or dry sherry
1 C	roughly chopped cilantro

1 Toast the cumin seeds and peppercorns in a dry skillet over medium heat until fragrant, about 1 minute. Pulse in a spice grinder until broken into pieces, but not finely ground. Mix the spices with the salt and chili flakes.

2 Toss the meat in the spice mixture, making sure every piece gets a good, even dusting of the spices.

3 Heat a very large skillet or wok over high heat. Add the oil, and when it emits wisps of smoke, add the onions and cook, tossing, until translucent around the edges, 1 to 2 minutes. Scoop the onions out of the wok and transfer to a bowl.

4 Add the lamb and any residual spices to the pan. Cook, tossing, until the meat begins to brown, about 2 minutes. Add the scallions, garlic, soy sauce, and wine, and bring to a brisk simmer. Keep tossing to coat the lamb in the sauce. After 2 to 3 minutes, when the lamb is just cooked through and coated in sauce, return the onions to the pan and toss everything together. Remove from the heat and fold in the cilantro. Serve hot.

Cumin and lamb are cozy bedfellows in a number of cuisines, but if they were putting together a scrapbook of their times and travels together, I think they'd choose this Chinese-style preparation as the goldenest of their golden years. It brings together so many old friends—garlic, onions, Sichuan peppercorns, dried red chili—but, like a great reunion episode of a sitcom, nobody lingers too long or tries to steal the spotlight.

Lamburgers

Makes 4 burgers

1 lb	ground lamb
1 T	ground cumin
1 t	Sichuan peppercorns, toasted and crushed
½ t	chili flakes
1½ t	kosher salt
1 T	neutral oil
1	small red onion, halved and thinly sliced
1	jalapeño or serrano chili, thinly sliced
4	potato hamburger buns
½ C	cilantro leaves

1 Combine the lamb, cumin, peppercorns, chili flakes, and salt in a bowl and mix with your hands. Form into 4 equal balls.

2 Heat the oil in a 12-inch cast iron skillet over medium-high heat. Add the onion and fresh chili and sear the vegetables until lightly browned around the edges but still crunchy, about 3 minutes.

3 Separate the vegetables into 4 equally sized and well-spaced mounds in the pan and top each with a ball of meat. Using the back of a large spatula, smash the meat into the vegetables, forming a ½-inch-thick patty. Sear the patty until the meat is opaque on the bottom ¼ inch, about 3 minutes. Flip and sear to desired doneness, about 3 minutes for medium.

4 Transfer the patties to buns and top with cilantro.

There are enough actual Chinese analogs to this sandwich to justify it, I think. (The sandwiches called *bing* come to mind, as do the lamb sandwiches that seem like they're jammed into the Chinese equivalent of pita.) But being American means never apologizing for burgerizing something, and that's what we've done here. A couple notes to the cook: You could mix the lamb with beef if you're into commingled meats. Even a 10 percent addition of lamb to a burger mix adds intrigue. And if you make these burgers on a grill, press the onions and peppers into the patties and grill that side first.

Thai-Style Lettuce Cups

Makes 4 servings

1 lb	ground pork, chicken, or turkey		**1 T**	neutral oil
2 T	minced lemongrass		**½ C**	thinly sliced red onion
1	garlic clove, grated		**½ C**	roughly chopped cilantro (leaves and stems)
½ t	kosher salt			
1 T	grated lime zest		**½ C**	roughly chopped mint leaves
3 T	fish sauce		**1**	head butter or romaine lettuce or ½ head white cabbage, leaves separated and washed
1 t	sambal oelek			
6 T	lime juice (about 3 limes)			
2 T	turbinado sugar			

1 Combine the meat, lemongrass, garlic, salt, lime zest, 1 tablespoon of the fish sauce, and ½ teaspoon of the sambal in a medium bowl. Mix with your hands or a spatula until thoroughly combined. Cover and chill until ready to use.

2 Whisk together the lime juice, sugar, and remaining 2 tablespoons fish sauce and ½ teaspoon sambal until the sugar dissolves. Set the sauce aside.

3 Heat the oil in a large skillet over medium-high heat. Add the meat mixture and cook, stirring and chopping it into fine pieces with a metal spatula or wooden spoon, until the meat is just cooked through, 5 to 6 minutes. Remove the pan from the heat and fold in the onion, cilantro, and mint. Scoop onto a plate or bowl and drizzle with the sauce. Serve with lettuce or cabbage leaves.

I wanted to put a *larb* in this book—larb being the spicy, acidic, flavor-bomb of an Isan salad that is all the rage these days in the ever-expanding American awareness of Thai cookery. But there were a few things that we couldn't ask you to do in the true spirit of ease; we couldn't call the results larb and still look at ourselves in the mirror in the morning. (It's weird to think about a whole group of people getting up and looking at themselves in the mirror, but that's how it is at *Lucky Peach*—we all live together and work in a loft that's kind of like the one in the first season of *The Real World*.)

So this dish, which is not larb, is larb-like, and pleasingly so. We tried making it with turkey to see if even the most pointless of ground meats could be elevated by this treatment, and we found it to work. But given the choice, pork is the champ.

Lion's Head Meatballs

Makes 4 servings

1 lb	ground pork (preferably very fatty; have your butcher grind pork belly, for example)	**½ t**	sesame oil
		1	large egg
		2 T	cornstarch
1 C	chopped scallions	**+**	neutral oil
2 T	soy sauce	**1 lb**	napa cabbage or bok choy, leaves separated, chopped if desired
1 T	sugar		
1 T	Shaoxing wine	**2 C**	chicken broth
1 T	minced garlic	**+**	white pepper
1 T	minced fresh ginger	**+**	cooked rice noodles or rice, for serving
1 t	kosher salt		

1 Put the pork in a large bowl and break it up with your hands. Add the scallions, soy sauce, sugar, wine, garlic, ginger, salt, and sesame oil and work the mixture to combine. Add the egg and cornstarch and vigorously mix, picking up and slapping the mixture back into the bowl a few times to create a tacky texture. Roll the meat into eight 2-inch balls.

2 Heat 1 tablespoon of oil in a Dutch oven and add enough meatballs to fit comfortably in a single layer. Sear them until browned all over, about 2 minutes per side. Repeat with any remaining meatballs. Remove the pan from the heat and wipe out the pan.

3 Line the pan with the cabbage or bok choy, arrange the meatballs in a snug single layer on top, and add broth to come within ¼ inch of the tops of the meatballs. Cover the pot and set over medium heat. Gently simmer until the greens are tender and the meatballs are cooked through, 20 to 30 minutes. Season to taste with white pepper and serve over rice noodles or with steamed rice.

The dish is sort of a stew but lighter: The meatballs, greens, and a little broth are all spooned over rice noodles. It's commonly known as lion's head meatballs, because the wavy greens or noodles ringing the meatballs look like . . . a lion's mane? Maybe if you squint.

In Chinese, they're called *shih tzu tou*, which the non-Chinese speakers among us can't help but see as shihtzu tou, so maybe they're really supposed to look like little lapdog heads. Even if they are taxonomically ambiguous, they are inarguably good eating.

Red Roast Pork

Makes 4 to 8 servings

¼ C	hoisin sauce		¼ C	Shaoxing wine or dry sherry
¼ C	soy sauce		1 t	Chinese five-spice powder
¼ C	honey		3 lbs	boneless pork shoulder

1 Whisk the hoisin, soy sauce, honey, wine, and five-spice together in a small bowl. Transfer the marinade to a zip-top bag.

For quick-cooking, crusty, slightly chewy char siu:

2a Slice the shoulder into ½-inch-thick slabs, then slice the slabs into 2-inch-long strips. Add to the marinade and marinate in the refrigerator for at least 12 hours and up to 48 hours.

3a Heat the oven to 400°F. Line a rimmed baking sheet with foil.

4a Remove the pork from the marinade, scraping off any excess. Lay the pork on a cooling rack or roasting rack set on the lined baking sheet. Roast for 15 minutes, then flip and roast until the fat is sizzling and the pork is cooked through, 10 to 15 minutes longer. Let rest a couple minutes before slicing and serving.

For shreddy, melty glazed pork shoulder:

2b Leave the meat in one piece, place it in the bag with the marinade, and marinate in the refrigerator for at least 24 hours and up to 48 hours. Remove from the refrigerator 1 hour before roasting.

3b Heat the oven to 300°F.

4b Set the pork in a roasting pan, reserving the marinade for basting. Roast the pork until the meat is completely tender, 4 to 5 hours, then baste with some of the reserved marinade. Continue roasting and basting every 10 minutes or so until the pork is coated in a thick, shiny glaze, about 1 hour longer. Remove from the oven and let rest 20 minutes before devouring.

Along with roast duck and crackly skinned pork, *char siu*—sweet, sticky, brick-red roast pork—is a fundamental part of Cantonese food, whether it's stuffed into pillowy steamed buns or sliced thin on top of noodles. The results of this char siu recipe are worthy of hanging from a metal hook in a neon-lit window in Chinatown. Cut the pork shoulder into strips for quick cooking and to maximize roasty, crusty, glazy bits, or leave it whole to make a glazed roast you can pull apart at the dinner table. With rice and one of the warm vegetables from pages 164 to 176, it's a feast.

Red Roast Pork
(shoulder)

Fish Sauce Spareribs

Makes 4 to 6 servings

2	racks spareribs (about 5 lbs; "St. Louis style" if available)	**2 T**	lime juice	
¾ C	fish sauce	**2 T**	minced fresh ginger	
1 C	sugar	**2 T**	minced garlic	
1 T	kosher salt	**2 t**	sambal oelek	
½ C	water	**1 t**	freshly ground black pepper	

1 Heat the oven to 350°F. Lay a large sheet of foil and then a large sheet of parchment paper on each of 2 rimmed baking sheets. (You're going to be wrapping each rack with them to create a packet, so make sure the sheets are long enough.)

2 Strip the papery membrane from the bone side of the ribs, if your butcher hasn't done this already. Lay each rack of ribs on its own baking sheet.

3 Whisk together ¼ cup of the fish sauce and ¼ cup of the sugar. Rub the mixture all over the ribs and arrange bone-side down on the parchment. Wrap with the parchment and foil, crimping the foil at the top.

4 Bake the ribs until tender but not falling apart, about 90 minutes. Remove from the oven and let rest in the foil for 30 minutes. Unwrap the ribs and pour any pan juices into a small bowl. At this point, the ribs can be rewrapped in foil and refrigerated up to 4 days. Store the pan juices in an airtight container.

5 If the ribs have been chilled, set them on a baking sheet (still in the foil) and reheat in a 350°F oven for 20 minutes.

6 Meanwhile, combine the salt, the remaining ¾ cup sugar, and the water in a medium saucepan set over medium-high heat. Add a couple drops of the lime juice and cook, swirling the pan occasionally until the syrup is homogeneously light amber, about 12 minutes. Remove the pan from the heat and add the ginger and garlic, swirling the pan (as opposed to stirring with a spoon, which will get trapped in the caramel) to gently combine the aromatics. Add the remaining lime juice and ½ cup fish sauce, sambal, and pepper and, once the bubbling subsides, stir to combine. The fish sauce caramel can be covered and chilled up to 2 weeks.

7 Heat the oven to 500°F. Line a baking sheet with foil.

8 Stir the reserved pan juices into the fish sauce caramel. Arrange the ribs meat-side up on the baking sheet and brush some of the caramel onto the ribs. Roast for 5 minutes, then baste with more caramel. Continue roasting and basting until most of the caramel is used up and the ribs have a sticky, shiny glaze, about 15 minutes. Remove from the oven and continue to baste for a few minutes, until the crust on the ribs cools and thickens slightly. Serve with plenty of napkins.

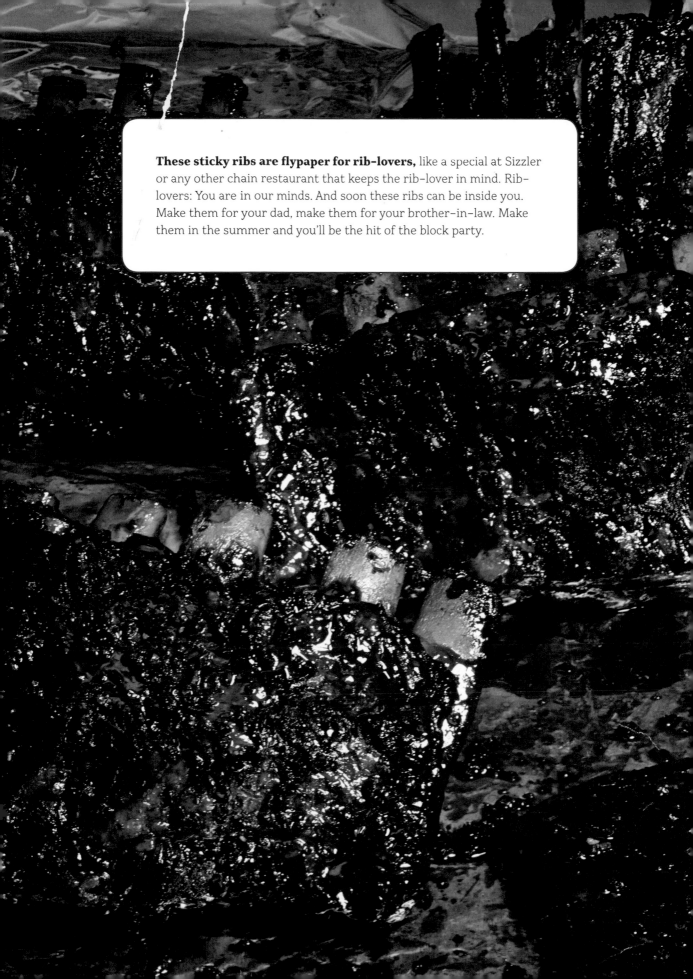

These sticky ribs are flypaper for rib-lovers, like a special at Sizzler or any other chain restaurant that keeps the rib-lover in mind. Rib-lovers: You are in our minds. And soon these ribs can be inside you. Make them for your dad, make them for your brother–in–law. Make them in the summer and you'll be the hit of the block party.

Macanese Pork Chop Bun

Makes 2 sandwiches

2	bone-in pork chops (½" thick, about 6 oz each)
1 t	minced garlic
+	kosher salt and freshly ground black pepper
+	neutral oil
+	butter, softened
2	Portuguese rolls, split

1 Whack the pork chops a couple of times with a mallet, a cleaver, or the bottom of a heavy saucepan to tenderize and flatten slightly. Rub with the garlic and season liberally with salt and pepper. Cover and marinate in the fridge for at least 1 hour and preferably overnight.

2 Heat ¼ inch of oil in a large heavy skillet over medium–high heat until it ripples. Lay the pork chops in the pan and press the bone into the hot oil, letting it sizzle for a few seconds. Fry the chops until they are cooked through and both sides are golden, about 3 minutes per side. Test the doneness by poking the center of the chop: The meat should bounce back and some juices will pool on the surface. Remove the pork from the pan and let the chops rest, stacked on top of each other, for a couple of minutes.

3 Pour the oil out of the skillet and wipe clean. Return to medium–low heat. Spread a little soft butter on the cut sides of the rolls. Toast the buttered bread in the skillet until evenly browned. Sandwich the pork chops in the toasted rolls and serve immediately. Chomp, then nibble until you are left with just a bone.

I don't hate pork chops. How could someone hate part of the pig? Even its ears are delicious. But pork chops get dry so easily—and dry pork is sadness in edible form. But not in these sandwiches, an emblematic Macanese street food: The meat stays moist and benefits from a lubricating layer of softened butter, and any juices that run out are absorbed into the bread. By the way, Portuguese rolls, which are soft but not trashy, are worth tracking down for the sandwich.

Pan-Roasted
Rib Eye with
Ms. Kwok's Black
Pepper Sauce
(page 224)

Pan-Roasted Rib Eye with Ms. Kwok's Black Pepper Sauce

Makes 2 to 4 servings

Ms. Kwok's black pepper sauce

1 T	neutral oil
2 t	freshly cracked black pepper
⅓ C	water
¼ C	soy sauce
2 t	sugar
+	kosher salt
2 t	cornstarch blended with 1 T water

Rib eye

1	rib eye (1½" thick, about 2 lbs)
2 t	kosher salt
1 T	neutral oil

1 Make the black pepper sauce: Heat the oil in a small saucepan over medium heat. Add the pepper and toast in the oil, swirling constantly, until the white insides of the peppercorn pieces are golden brown. (This is a critical stage in flavor development. Don't be a dingus. Do not skip this step!)

2 Stir in the water, soy sauce, and sugar. Bring to a boil and taste it. Like, actually taste it. Add a pinch of salt if needed, or dilute the sauce with a splash of water if it strikes you as salty. Maybe it needs another pinch of sugar? The sauce should be spicy and a touch sweet. Once the seasoning is correct, whisk in the cornstarch mixture and return it to a boil. Boil for 1 minute, then remove from the heat. The sauce will keep for 1 week in the fridge. Rewarm before serving.

3 Cook the rib eye: Heat the oven to 400°F.

4 Season the steak with the salt. Heat the oil in a large cast iron skillet over high heat. When a wisp of smoke rises from the pan, lay the steak in, and sear until a brown crust forms, about 2 minutes. Flip and sear 2 minutes longer. Pick up the steak with your tongs and carefully roll the edge of the steak in the pan, rendering the fat cap. Your steak should be browned and crusty all over. Lay the steak back down on a broad side and carefully transfer the pan to the oven.

5 Roast, flipping halfway through, until the internal temperature reaches 120°F, about 8 minutes total. Let it rest for at least 10 minutes before carving into thin slices. Serve with Ms. Kwok's black pepper sauce.

If this recipe were a song, it would be one of those Jay-Z verses that just brags endlessly about how awesome and rich it is. And those facts, whether about him or this meat, check out.

Mary-Frances Heck, who helped create the recipes in this book from ideas scribbled on napkins and family recipes stored in our musty brain buckets, scored this sauce recipe from her friend Bary's mom, Ms. Cathy Kwok, who brought it with her from Hong Kong to Massachusetts.

Whether or not you dress the steak like we do here, this is also a great technique for cooking steak at home and getting it right every time. Also, the Asian wedge salad (see page 248) is a dead simple and perfect companion to a fat piece of meat like this.

Note: Cooking a steak of this size to medium-rare takes 15 minutes of active cooking time. Don't skimp on the sear because you think you need to roast it for a certain length of time. Set a timer for 15 minutes. Start it when the steak hits the pan. Sear it properly, then roast it for the remainder of the 15 minutes, flipping about halfway through. If your pan is hot and oven preheated, the timing will work.

Seafood

Tod Mun Fish Cakes

Makes 2 main-course or 4 appetizer servings

Fish cakes

12 oz	fresh cod or other mild white fish, cut into 1" pieces
¼ C	red curry paste
1	large egg
1 T	fish sauce
1 T	sugar
½ t	kosher salt

Sauce

½ C	Thai sweet chili sauce
1 C	chopped seeded cucumber
2 T	chopped roasted unsalted peanuts
2 T	minced cilantro
1 t	sambal oelek (optional)
+	lime juice or salt
+	neutral oil
+	lime wedges, for serving

1 Make the fish cakes: Pulse the fish, curry paste, egg, fish sauce, sugar, and salt in a food processor until nearly smooth and a few pea-size pieces of fish remain. Cover and refrigerate until ready to cook, up to 24 hours.

2 Meanwhile, make the sauce: Mix together the chili sauce, cucumber, peanuts, cilantro, and sambal (if using). Let stand 15 minutes for the cucumbers to weep some of their juices. Stir and adjust the seasoning with a squeeze of lime or pinch of salt.

3 When you're ready to fry the fish cakes, heat ⅛ inch oil in a large heavy skillet. Roll 2 tablespoons of the fish mixture into a ball and pat it into a ¾-inch-thick cake. Working in batches, fry the cakes, flipping once, until golden and a little puffed, about 4 minutes per side. Blot on paper towels and serve hot, with the sauce and lime wedges.

This is one of those kick-off-the-meal dishes I always order at Thai places (it's a staple of first-wave and central Thai restaurants of the United States, less common at your Isan and northern Thai spots). When that mix of kaffir lime from the curry paste in the fish cake and crisp cucumber in the sweet-and-spicy goo get to mingling, I think warm self-congratulatory thoughts. *What a good dish. What a good order. Aren't we glad we came here? Life is good.* Then the pad Thai is vacant and bland and it takes forever to get home on the train and life goes back to being the parade of minor insults it usually is.

So why not subtract the guesswork and make it at home? It's shamefully easy. We have omitted kaffir lime from the ingredient list here since it's hard to find (look in the freezer case at a Southeast Asian grocery store if you have access to one) and since it's usually in the red curry paste anyway. If you've got it, add a leaf to the purée.

Ms. Vo Thi Huong's Garlic Shrimp

Makes 4 servings

3 T	neutral oil
6	garlic cloves, roughly chopped
1	large shallot, roughly chopped
2	bunches (12–14) scallions, cut into 2" lengths
1 lb	large shrimp, shelled and deveined
1 T	sriracha sauce (or more to taste)
2 T	Kewpie mayonnaise
2 T	soy sauce
+	cooked jasmine rice, for serving

1 Heat the oil in a wok over medium-high heat. After a minute, add the garlic, shallot, and scallions and stir-fry for 1 minute.

2 Add the shrimp to the pan and stir-fry until the shrimp are no longer translucent and beginning to brown in spots, 2 to 3 minutes.

3 Briskly stir in the sriracha, mayonnaise, and soy sauce. Toss to bring the sauce elements together and coat the shrimp and vegetables. Remove from the heat and serve hot with rice.

Writer Laurie Woolever brought this recipe back to us from the white-sand beaches of Hue, Vietnam, where a lady named Ms. Vo Thi Huong stir-fries fresh shrimp like these. Shrimp in hot mayonnaise may sound bad when you call it that, but the truth is in the eating. Serve with white rice and cold beer.

Miso-Roasted Fish

Makes 4 servings

¼ C	mirin
¼ C	sake
½ C	white miso
¼ C	sugar
2 lbs	fish fillets (preferably skin on), pin bones removed
+	neutral oil

1 Pour the mirin and sake into a small saucepan and bring to a boil. Boil for 1 minute, then remove from the heat and whisk in the miso. This will take some effort and determination, but make sure the mixture is completely smooth before stirring in the sugar. Return to the heat and stir until the sugar is dissolved and the mixture is homogenous. Let the marinade cool. It will keep in the fridge for a couple of weeks.

2 Combine the cooled marinade with the fish fillets in a zip-top bag. Any amount of marination from 1 to 72 hours is okay (it's still safe after that, it's just that the marinade completely takes over). We've found 48 hours in the fridge to be the sweet spot.

3 Heat the oven to 400°F.

4 Remove the fish from the marinade; wipe off and discard any excess. Heat a few drops of oil in an ovenproof skillet. Working in batches if necessary to not crowd the pan, sear the fish fillets flesh-side down until browned and the miso crust is set, 1 to 2 minutes. Flip them seared-side up and slide into the oven.

5 Roast until the fish is opaque and flaky, 6 to 10 minutes depending on the thickness of the fillets. A paring knife or skewer should meet no resistance when the flesh is pierced. Let the fish rest for a minute (or longer, it's perfectly good at room temperature) and serve.

This has been my go-to move for when I see fish I want to eat but I already have other dinner plans or dinners planned. I grab the fish from the farmers' market, throw them in a bag with this marinade, and when Tuesday night rolls around and I think, *What's for dinner?*, the fish speaks up and says, "Me." Except for the fish is not talking because I don't live in Pee-wee's Playhouse and it doesn't have a mouth because it's a fillet so how would it talk anyway?

I usually do this with white-fleshed fish like cod or black bass, because they're available where I live, and because the most famous rendition of this fairly classic Japanese preparation is done with firm, white-fleshed fish by Nobu Matsuhisa. But in a low-risk scientific trial, we found that it's an exceedingly good way to cook all kinds of fish: oily, bony, big, or otherwise.

Coco-Curried Mussels

Makes 2 to 4 servings

1 T	neutral oil
3 T	Thai green curry paste
1	can (14 oz) coconut milk
1 T	palm, raw, or light brown sugar
2 lbs	mussels, rinsed
+	kosher salt
1 T	fish sauce
½ C	roughly chopped cilantro
1	small green chili, such as serrano or jalapeño, thinly sliced
+	lime wedges, for squeezing
+	crusty baguette, for serving

1 Heat the oil in a lidded Dutch oven or 4-quart saucepan over medium heat. Add the curry paste and fry until very fragrant, about 1 minute. Stir in the coconut milk and sugar and bring to a simmer.

2 Add the mussels and a pinch of salt, folding once or twice to coat and cover tightly with a lid. Simmer until the mussels have opened, 6 to 8 minutes. Discard any mussels that do not open.

3 Stir in the fish sauce and sprinkle with cilantro and chili. Serve with lime wedges for squeezing and bread for sopping up.

Mantras for (These) Mussels
Mussels are cheap and easy.
Mussels are cheap and easy.
Sometimes canned food is your friend.
Sometimes canned food is your friend.
A pile of herbs, chilies, and citrus adds vigor.
A pile of herbs, chilies, and citrus adds vigor.
Don't forget the baguette!
Don't forget the baguette!

Clams with Lemongrass in a Vietnamese Style

Makes 2 servings

24	littleneck clams
½ C	kosher salt
1 T	oil
2	stalks lemongrass, whacked with the broad side of a knife
½ C	sliced shallots
½ C	pieces (2") celery
2	garlic cloves, sliced
4	slices (¼" thick) fresh ginger
6	small dried red chilies
2 C	water
1	lemon, quartered and thinly sliced
1	plum tomato, chopped (about ½ C)
¼ C	pieces (1") cilantro stems
1 T	fish sauce, plus more as needed
1 t	sambal oelek
1 t	palm, raw, or light brown sugar, plus more as needed
+	crusty baguette, for serving

1 To purge the clams, rinse them, then submerge in a large bowl of water. Add the salt. Refrigerate for at least 1 hour. Remove the clams from the brine and rinse. Set aside.

2 Heat the oil in a large saucepan or medium Dutch oven over medium heat. Add the lemongrass, shallots, celery, garlic, ginger, and chilies and sweat until slightly softened, 2 to 3 minutes.

3 Increase the heat to high, fold in the clams, and add the water. Cover and simmer until the clams open, 6 to 8 minutes. Discard any clams that do not open.

4 Stir in the lemon, tomato, cilantro stems, fish sauce, sambal, and sugar. Taste and adjust the seasoning with additional fish sauce or sugar. Serve hot, with baguette.

Three things are right about this dish: the interplay of briny clams and the ethereal-fairy flavor of lemongrass; the gentle but assured acidity imparted by the tomatoes and lime; the fact that it's an excuse to eat a whole baguette soaked in that delicious broth.

Kung Pao Shrimp

Makes 2 to 4 servings

Sauce

2 T	water
1 T	soy sauce
1 T	Shaoxing wine
1 T	Chinkiang vinegar
1 T	sugar
1 t	sesame oil
1 t	cornstarch
+	pinch of white pepper

Stir-fry

3 T	neutral oil
10	small dried red chilies
1 t	Sichuan peppercorns
2 t	minced garlic
2 t	minced fresh ginger
½	red bell pepper, cut into ½" pieces
½	green bell pepper, cut into ½" pieces
2	celery stalks, cut into ½" pieces
1 lb	large shrimp, shelled and deveined
+	kosher salt
2	scallions, cut into 1" pieces
½ C	roasted unsalted peanuts
+	cooked rice, for serving

1 Make the sauce: Whisk together the sauce ingredients in a small bowl until the cornstarch is dissolved. Set aside.

2 Make the stir-fry: Heat 2 tablespoons of the oil in a wok over high heat. Add the chilies and peppercorns and stir-fry until they puff and brown slightly, about 5 seconds. Add the garlic, ginger, and bell peppers and stir-fry until the peppers are browned in spots and crisp-tender, about 1 minute. Using a slotted spoon, transfer the mixture to a plate. Add the celery to the pan and stir-fry until heated through and charred in spots, about 2 minutes. Transfer to the plate with the peppers.

3 Add the remaining 1 tablespoon oil to the wok. Season the shrimp with salt and add to the wok. Stir-fry until almost cooked through, about 3 minutes. Return the peppers, celery, and spices to the wok. Add the scallions and peanuts and toss to combine everything. Add the sauce and cook, stirring, until it bubbles and thickens. When the sauce is thick and the shrimp are cooked through, remove from the heat. Serve with rice.

Kung Pao (or *gung bao*) dishes are a celebration of texture, a cascade of crunchy, slippery, and crisp that keeps every bite interesting. We've made two tweaks to the classic: We dialed the heat all the way down and swapped out the more common chicken for shrimp. The shrimp substitution we stand by; the chili heat is your call and very easy to ramp up.

Squid and Grapefruit Salad

Makes 2 main-course salads

2 T	fish sauce
1 T	sugar, plus more to taste
1 t	sambal oelek
1	garlic clove, minced
2	fresh red chilies, sliced
1	lime, halved
1	large pink grapefruit
8 oz	cleaned squid, bodies scored, tentacles quartered lengthwise
¼ C	loosely packed mint leaves
+	cooked rice (preferably sticky rice), for serving

1 Bring a medium pot of water to a boil.

2 Meanwhile, stir together the fish sauce, sugar, sambal, chilies, and garlic in a medium bowl until the sugar dissolves. Squeeze in the juice of a lime half. Cut the other lime half into wedges for serving.

3 Cut off the peel and pith of the grapefruit. Working over a bowl, slice between the grapefruit's membranes, releasing the segments into the bowl. Once all of the segments are free, squeeze the membranes to release juices into the bowl.

4 Blanch the squid in the boiling water until it curls and turns opaque, about 30 seconds. Remove with a spider and transfer to the bowl with the fish sauce vinaigrette. Toss to coat and let cool slightly.

5 Once the squid cools, drain the grapefruit segments from the juice and add to the squid, breaking up any large pieces into smaller bites. Toss everything in the vinaigrette, adding more grapefruit juice or sugar as needed to balance the sweet-sourness.

6 Tear the mint into the bowl with the squid and toss. Serve with rice and add the lime wedges.

Laurie Woolever brought back this dish from the same trip to Vietnam that gave us the saucy, guilty-pleasure garlic shrimp on page 230. This salad is that dish's diametric opposite: sharp, clean, and acidic. Originally made with the giant grapefruit–like pomelo fruit, this seafood–citrus combo is often found in Southeast Asia: *yum som o, thanh tra, goi buoi tom thit.*

If you've got a grill, grill the whole squid over an ungodly hot fire until it's charred and just cooked, then chop it up and toss it in the vinaigrette in step 4.

Steamed Whole Fish, Two Sauces

Makes 2 servings

1	whole white-fleshed fish (about 1¼ lbs), scaled, gutted, and rinsed	**+**	SAUCE (recipes follow)
		+	cooked rice, for serving

1 Pat the fish dry. Have your **SAUCE** ingredients at the ready.

2 Bring 2 inches of water to a boil in a wok or pot fitted with a steamer. Lay the fish on your choice of steamer contraption and cover the wok or pan with a tight-fitting lid. Steam for 8 minutes. Transfer the fish to a serving platter.

3 Dump out the water and wipe your wok clean. Prepare your chosen **SAUCE** recipe. Serve with plenty of rice.

This recipe follows what I think of as the Cantonese-seafood-restaurant principle: You pick the freshest fish, cook it simply, and sauce it simply.

PICK IT Make this dish when you have great whole fish available routinely or because something at the fish counter was looking very freshly killed.

COOK IT I recommend steaming here, but you could absolutely bake the fish on a cooling rack set on a baking sheet at 400°F for 15-ish minutes, or grill it.

SAUCE IT Here are two sauces I particularly like over whole fish, but the sky's the limit.

Triple S: Soy-Sauce Sauce

2 T	neutral oil	2 T	brown sugar
2 T	julienned fresh ginger	¼ t	sesame oil
		⅛ t	white pepper
¼ C	soy sauce	2 T	water
2 T	Shaoxing wine	¼ C	sliced scallions

1 Arrange the ginger on the cooked fish. Heat the neutral oil in the wok over high heat until it smokes. Pour the hot oil over the fish. Everything should sizzle and the fish's skin will tighten and glisten.

2 Return the wok to the flame and pour in the soy sauce and wine. Stir in the sugar, sesame oil, pepper, and water. When it bubbles, pour the sauce over the fish and sprinkle with the scallions.

Black Bean Sauce

2 T	neutral oil	¼ C	soy sauce
2 T	minced garlic	2 T	Shaoxing wine
2 T	minced fresh ginger	2 T	water
		2 T	sugar
2 T	fermented black beans, rinsed		

1 Heat the neutral oil in the wok over high heat until it smokes. Pour the hot oil over the fish. The fish's skin will tighten and glisten.

2 Return the wok to the flame and add the garlic, ginger, and black beans and stir-fry for 15 seconds. Add the soy sauce, wine, water, and sugar and bring to a boil. Pour over the fish.

Serve these sauces
with a lot of jasmine
rice and one of the
warm vegetables on
pages 164 to 176.

Super Sauces

Danny Bowien's Ginger-Scallion Sauce

Makes about ½ cup

1 T	grapeseed or other neutral oil
1 C	thinly sliced scallions
1 C	finely minced fresh ginger
1½ t	kosher salt
1½ T	fish sauce
1 t	turbinado sugar
¼ t	white pepper

1 Heat the oil in a large skillet over high heat until the oil emits wisps of smoke. Add the scallions and ginger to the pan and immediately remove from the heat, stirring until no longer sizzling.

2 Transfer the wilted scallions and ginger to a small bowl and season with the salt, fish sauce, sugar, and white pepper. Ginger–scallion sauce keeps, covered and refrigerated, for up to 2 days.

Dave Chang's Ginger-Scallion Sauce

Makes about 1 cup

1¼ C	thinly sliced scallions
¼ C	finely minced fresh ginger
2 T	grapeseed or other neutral oil
1 t	soy sauce
½ t	sherry vinegar
½ t	kosher salt

Mix together the scallions, ginger, oil, soy sauce, vinegar, and salt in a bowl. Taste and check for salt, adding more if needed. Though it's best after 15 or 20 minutes of sitting, the ginger–scallion sauce is good from the minute it's stirred together up to a day or two in the fridge. Use as directed, or apply as needed.

The uses for ginger-scallion sauce are limited only by imagination or the outer limits of desire: If you boil noodles and toss them in it, you have dinner. It makes leftover vegetables and a bowl of rice sparkle like something concocted with intention. Roast chicken pines for it; baked fish can't get enough.

In making it, there are nearly as many methods as there are cooks. I've singled out two here, because they represent different ends of the spectrum. Chang's is simple and raw, for lack of a better term. Many versions of the sauce call for heating the oil before adding it to the aromatics (not a bad idea) or briefly cooking the aromatics first (if you're inclined, try Bowien's). The result is a bold, direct, two-fisted sauce that stands out in finished dishes. I copped Danny Bowien's ginger-scallion sauce recipe when he showed me how to make the lamb dumplings that Mission Chinese Food periodically puts on its menu—the ginger-scallion sauce goes in the dumplings as one of the many components of the dish. His is slightly more complicated to make (by a measure of a few minutes) and more complex as a finished sauce: salty, umami, a sweet finish. On one hand, making ginger-scallion sauce just to shove it in some dumplings felt like a lot of work—two recipes, one product. But then, like the kid leaning against the bookcase that turns out to be the entrance to the secret underground maze, it made me think: Not only can you put ginger-scallion sauce on things, you can put it in things. Like if you had some leftover GS sauce around, maybe that would do all the dumpling-seasoning work—and, sure enough, it did! You can make the Dollar Dumplings (page 60) with nothing more than 3 leftover tablespoons of sauce. Or you can stir a couple spoonfuls into mayonnaise and practically open your own artisanal sandwich shop with whatever creation you put it on.

Carrot-Ginger Dressing

Makes 1 cup

1	piece (2") fresh ginger, sliced
1	small carrot, roughly chopped (about ¼ C)
¼ C	roughly chopped onion
2 T	rice vinegar
1 T	soy sauce
½ t	sugar
1 t	sesame oil
¼ C	vegetable oil
+	kosher salt

With the motor running, toss the ginger and carrot into a blender. Add the onion, vinegar, soy sauce, and sugar, and process until smooth. Slowly drizzle in the sesame oil and vegetable oil and blend until emulsified. Season lightly with salt. The dressing will keep, covered and refrigerated, for 1 week.

You might know this dressing from such places as Benihana or the vaguely Asian, mainly vegetarian restaurant everybody started going to freshman year of college. It rules. Making a chopped salad with a bunch of supermarket vegetables that look like they were sprung from the soil at Chernobyl? This dressing's got you covered. It works as a dip, too, for blanched or raw vegetables. Jokingly we said that you could turn any vegetable into salad simply by anointing it with a hit of the orange stuff, and when we poured some onto the wedge of napa cabbage in the photo of Pan-Roasted Rib Eye (page 224), it turned out to be true: napa cabbage + this salad dressing = very delicious. The possibilities are endless.

Octo Vinaigrette

Makes 1 cup

2 T	finely chopped garlic
2 T	chopped fresh ginger
¼ t	chili flakes, or more to taste
¼ C	rice vinegar
¼ C	soy sauce
2 T	neutral oil
¼ t	sesame oil
1½ T	sugar
+	freshly ground black pepper

Combine the garlic, ginger, chili flakes, vinegar, soy sauce, grapeseed oil, sesame oil, sugar, and a few turns of black pepper in a lidded container, and shake well to mix. This will keep in the fridge for 4 to 5 days, and is good on everything except ostrich eggs.

This is an old favorite of mine, a recipe devised by Kevin Pemoulie, now the chef–owner of Thirty Acres in Jersey City, New Jersey, but then the chef de cuisine of Momofuku Noodle Bar. Chang and I first published it in the *Momofuku* cookbook. As its name implies, it was originally devised for octopus, but it was later used over Noodle Bar's first fried chicken. (They've since gone away from that, but IMLTHO, fried chicken is tops topped with this. And, subparenthetically, it is also very good with the seasoning packet from instant ramen shaken all over it. But I digress.) ANYHOW, this is one of those over–any–protein sauces that international condiment conglomerates would murder each other to patent, but here it is free and easy for you to enjoy. This + anything grilled/most things fried = winning at eating.

Nuoc Cham

½ C	fish sauce
¼ C	water
¼ C	lime juice
2 T	palm, raw, or light brown sugar
1	garlic clove, minced
½ t	sambal oelek

Combine the fish sauce, water, lime juice, sugar, garlic, and sambal. Adjust the consistency with a little more water, if very thick, or more sambal if you like it spicy. Nuoc cham keeps, refrigerated, for up to 1 week.

If Vietnamese cuisine was a car, this would be the juice it ran on. It is the fundamental condiment. On poorly planned or just low-money nights, proud men have been known to eat it over rice and call that dinner. There is no Vietnamese meal at which this wouldn't be welcome at the table and/or spooned into or onto something eventually.

Sambal

Makes ½ cup

8 oz	fresh red chilies (such as Holland, Fresno, or finger)
2 t	kosher salt
2 T	distilled white vinegar

1 Chop the chilies and place in a mortar with the salt and grind to a paste. (If you don't have a mortar and pestle, grate the chilies on a Microplane or on the fine side of a box grater into a bowl. Stir the salt into the pulp and let stand until dissolved, about 10 minutes.)

2 Cover with a cheesecloth and let stand at room temperature until little bubbles form, 24 to 48 hours. Stir in the vinegar. Transfer to an airtight container. Refrigerated, this keeps for 2 weeks.

There is no question about whether store-bought sambal oelek is great. (Much like Hall & Oates's *Greatest Hits*, there's just no arguing about that.) But it doesn't mean you can't make some yourself.

I'm sure somebody's gonna make it with Thai bird peppers or some competition/show pepper and make it hot enough to singe your eyebrows off, but I'd advise shopping on the milder end of the hot chili department. I like hot sauce with more or less everything, but I don't wanna look like the guy in *The Wall* after eating it.

Use it in place of commercially made sambal oelek called for anywhere in this book or to spice up whatever you're eating. And don't be shy about dressing it up to go with the food you're serving it with—stir in a squeeze of lime, grated garlic, or sugar (½ teaspoon is a good place to start), or mix it with equal parts white vinegar to turn it into a dashable hot sauce.

Tofu Dressing

Makes a scant 2 cups

½ C	silken tofu
¼ C	soy sauce
1 T	sugar
1 T	sambal oelek
1 T	sherry vinegar
1½ t	sesame oil
½ C	canola oil

Combine the tofu, soy sauce, sugar, sambal, vinegar, and sesame oil in a blender. Blend until smooth. With the motor running, drizzle in the canola oil; the dressing will become the consistency of loose pudding. Tofu dressing keeps, covered and refrigerated, for up to 1 week.

In the early days of Má Pêche, the Momofuku restaurant in midtown Manhattan, this dressing appeared on a late-summer salad of barely cooked beans—I think it was a mix of all the beautiful varieties that fill the market just before the weather turns cold and we head back to rutabaga season here in New York.

I immediately removed it from that context and started using it willy-nilly at home. It was good on everything: The flavors of the sambal and sesame oil and vinegar and sugar all take their turns at center stage, stretching out the pleasure of eating it. It works poured over vegetables or as a dip. It has an I Can't Believe It's Not Butter quality to it, in that "tofu sauce" is not something that sounds even remotely good said out loud—but the tofu and oil make for something both crazy—creamy and pleasingly light.

Odd Flavor Sauce

Makes about ½ cup

3 T	soy sauce
2 T	tahini or almond or peanut butter
1 T	Chinkiang vinegar (preferable!) or red-wine vinegar
1 T	sesame oil
2 t	sugar
¼ t	kosher salt
3 T	neutral oil
1	small scallion, finely chopped (about 1 T)
1 T	minced fresh ginger
1	large garlic clove, finely chopped (about 1 t)
½ t	chili flakes, or more to taste
½ t	crushed Sichuan peppercorns

1 Combine the soy sauce, tahini, vinegar, sesame oil, sugar, and salt in a small heatproof bowl and mix until the sugar is dissolved and the tahini is well incorporated. (It might not be perfectly dissolved. That's okay.)

2 Heat a small skillet over medium heat, add the neutral oil, swirl, and heat until shimmering. Toss in the scallion, ginger, garlic, chili flakes, and crushed peppercorns. Remove from the heat and stir for 10 seconds, until the scallion is bright green and the mixture is very aromatic. Pour the contents of the pan into the liquid seasonings, whisking until well blended. Once cool, this sauce will keep in the fridge for a day or two.

I acquired my first copy of Irene Kuo's *The Key to Chinese Cooking* from a used bookstore and soon enough homed in on her recipe for Odd-Flavored Sauce, which appealed to me because it had everything in it: chili heat, peppercorn punch, the sting of black vinegar, the warm charm of sesame oil. What's not to like?

We've dialed in her recipe a little more to our taste. It is good with any warm white proteins—your chicken, fish, pork, and tofu—and can generally bring life to any bland food straight out of the fridge. Salt-and-pepper one of those proteins and heat through until it's cooked (in a pan, in the toaster oven, whatever), slice it up, douse it in the Odd Flavor, and (with a little rice) dinner is done.

Dessert

Oranges

One orange per person? Unless they're really good. Then you'll want more.

+   oranges

Cut them up or don't.

There is some minor degree of facetiousness in running a recipe for oranges. But I don't want you to feel like even 0.9900990099 percent of this compilation is here to do anything other than to make for easier cooking and a harder time fitting into non-elastic pants.

The deal with dessert in the scheme of easy Asian cooking is that you are NOT MAKING IT, not in the "easy" French way of throwing together a last-minute clafoutis. You are serving fruit. Cut-up fruit if you've got the time.

Korean moms are melon-slingers: cantaloupe and watermelon. Seasons be damned, there's gonna be melon. Fruits like mangoes are so good in the tropical environments they grow in that how could you not want some to finish off your Thai dinner?

Joanne Chang, pastry chef/co-owner of Flour Bakery and Myers + Chang in Boston, told us, "My parents would invite friends over, and my brother and I would help as much as we could and be excited because we'd get foods that we didn't usually get," which meant mainly that "at dessert time there would be this huge platter of oranges. So for me, that was dessert, that was how you ended a meal: with fruit.

"You know, sometimes they would sex up the fruit a little bit and use pineapple or melon or whatever happened to be in season. I can only speak for Taiwanese culture—I'm Taiwanese—but we don't have sweet tooths."

This is true and not true. Sweets are a huge part of the Asian culinary canon, but they are very often made and purchased outside of the home: bakeries are community hubs; baked goods are often part of daytime meals that go with tea.

And here's the thing: Nobody nowhere argues with sweets at the end of the meal. Fruit is the healthiest and easiest choice. But there's no shame in the game of getting bakery cakes, frozen mochi at the Japanese market, and serving it in a minorly elegant way—whether it's orange wedges or green tea Kit Kats—it's the gesture that counts the most.

Egg Custard Tarts

Makes 12 servings

⅓ C	sugar
⅓ C	water
2	large eggs
½ C	milk
¼ t	vanilla extract
+	kosher salt
1	package (about 1 lb) frozen puff pastry, thawed
+	all-purpose flour

1 Heat the oven to 350°F. Have a muffin tin at the ready.

2 Dissolve the sugar in the water in a small bowl. Whisk in the eggs, milk, vanilla, and a pinch of salt.

3 Unfold the puff pastry on a lightly floured work surface. Roll to a ⅛-inch thickness, then punch out 3-inch (big enough to line your molds) circles with a biscuit cutter or drinking glass. Press the dough into the molds, trimming off excess. Dock the pastry (prick it with a fork) more than you think you should.

4 Bake the pastry for 10 minutes, so it is slightly puffed and hard to the touch but not at all browned. Remove from the oven and gently press back any dough that has bubbled out. Leave the oven on, but reduce the temperature to 325°F.

5 Divide the custard among the tart shells. Return to the oven and bake until the custards are set, 25 to 30 minutes. Remove and let cool completely before eating.

Even if I'm going with EAT FRUIT as *Lucky Peach*'s easy Asian dessert mantra, I can't pretend like there aren't people with an unnatural fixation on baking out there (like my wife) or a fixation on egg tarts (like my oldest daughter, who will eat two orders of them at dim sum without even pretending like she's going to share any).

A few notes: We're using milk instead of condensed milk here, because it makes a lighter custard. Also, cheap puff pastry is easier to work with and produces more even, reliable results than hyperbuttery artisanal or homemade dough. We're not specifying a mold shape since this recipe will work in a muffin tin. Just be sure to dock the pastry well.

Acknowledgments

Trying to compose the appropriate thanks for a collectively assembled book like this one is impossible. Where to stop? I consulted Jonathan Gold on an early rendition of Gado Gado when we were getting recipes together, and his consternation at what I proposed helped me push our recipe so far from its roots as to turn a salad into a dip. Should I thank Shuen Kee Chong, who taught twenty-year-old me how to shop in Chinatown and introduced me to much of this cooking? Or Miki Tanaka, a stalwart friend of the last couple of decades, who makes it seem like I know stuff about Japanese food when, in fact, I just have the phone number of someone who does? Yes, yes, and yes. Thanks to them, and to all the people, chefs and authors, eaters and readers, who've helped shape, shift, or shove the ideas in this book to the places they needed to be.

But on the real-specific-making-of-this-book tip: Mary-Frances Heck's unflusterable manner and resolute commitment to the actual, functional doability of recipes was super-duper essential to whatever is good about what's between these covers.

Gabriele Stabile, Mark Ibold, and Hannah Clark did real dream weaver's work with the propping, styling, and shooting of all the photos in this book. They killed some dumb ideas and took other ones to new and exciting levels of stupidity. Their talent brings the book to life.

Walter Green and Helen Tseng created and executed the handsome design here and dealt with endless last-minute requests. In fact, no requests they dealt with were ever conveyed with any less than wild-eyed late-night urgency, and the fact that they turned every sour mango of an art problem into a gemlike ripe rambutan of quality book design without stabbing anybody in the eye is extraordinary and commendable. Jason Polan's drawings brought eleventh-hour levity and joy to the bookmaking process and added a humanizing dimension to the pages. He's the best; you should seek out his other work.

I have submitted a requisition form to supply Rica Allannic and her team at Clarkson Potter with a variety of deluxe foot spas, massaging chair inserts, and Ayurvedic healing balms: Marysarah Quinn, Christine Tanigawa, and Derek Gullino. They deserve them.

And then there's the edit team at *Lucky Peach*, who helped shape the manuscript, who helped select the recipes, who contributed some and edited all. Joanna Sciarrino bore the brunt of bringing all the pieces together, which I imagine was like working in the ER on the Island of Misfit Toys: Everything was already broken, but she found ways to fix them up regardless. Chris Ying, Rachel Khong, and Brette Warshaw brought careful eyes to the manuscript. They are all awesome and better people than the people at your magazine, so take that.

Lastly, personally: Thanks to Kim Witherspoon, who is mean or nice at exactly the right times. And, most important, thanks to Hannah and Hazel and Joni, my family, for making and letting this book happen. We didn't get the *Lucky Peach* test kitchen built in time to do this book, so photo shoots and recipe development all happened in my apartment, which at night often smelled like the inside of a wok. They were endlessly patient and encouraging and I love them even more than I love Cumin Lamb (page 208), which is saying a lot because I ate that entire multiperson portion in the photo only minutes after the picture was taken.

—PFM, 2015

Index

Conversion Chart
Equivalent Imperial and Metric Measurements

American cooks use standard containers, the 8-ounce cup and a tablespoon that takes exactly 16 level fillings to fill that cup level. Measuring by cup makes it very difficult to give weight equivalents, as a cup of densely packed butter will weigh considerably more than a cup of flour. The easiest way therefore to deal with cup measurements in recipes is to take the amount by volume rather than by weight. Thus the equation reads:

1 cup = 240 ml = 8 fl. oz.
½ cup = 120 ml = 4 fl. oz.

It is possible to buy a set of American cup measures in major stores around the world.

In the States, butter is often measured in sticks. One stick is the equivalent of 8 tablespoons. One tablespoon of butter is therefore the equivalent to ½ ounce / 15 grams.

Liquid Measures

Fluid Ounces	U.S.	Imperial	Milliliters
	1 teaspoon	1 teaspoon	5
¼	2 teaspoons	1 dessertspoon	10
½	1 tablespoon	1 tablespoon	14
1	2 tablespoons	2 tablespoons	28
2	¼ cup	4 tablespoons	56
4	½ cup		120
5		¼ pint or 1 gill	140
6	¾ cup		170
8	1 cup		240
9			250, ¼ liter
10	1¼ cups	½ pint	280
12	1½ cups		340
15		¾ pint	420
16	2 cups		450
18	2¼ cups		500, ½ liter
20	2½ cups	1 pint	560
24	3 cups		675
25		1¼ pints	700
27	3½ cups		750
30	3¾ cups	1½ pints	840
32	4 cups or 1 quart		900
35		1¾ pints	980
36	4½ cups		1000, 1 liter
40	5 cups	2 pints or 1 quart	1120

Solid Measures

U.S. and Imperial Measures		Metric Measures	
Ounces	Pounds	Grams	Kilos
1		28	
2		56	
3½		100	
4	¼	112	
5		140	
6		168	
8	½	225	
9		250	¼
12	¾	340	
16	1	450	
18		500	½
20	1¼	560	
24	1½	675	
27		750	¾
28	1¾	780	
32	2	900	
36	2¼	1000	1
40	2½	1100	
48	3	1350	
54		1500	1½

Oven Temperature Equivalents

Fahrenheit	Celsius	Gas Mark	Description
225	110	¼	Cool
250	130	½	
275	140	1	Very Slow
300	150	2	
325	170	3	Slow
350	180	4	Moderate
375	190	5	
400	200	6	Moderately Hot
425	220	7	Fairly Hot
450	230	8	Hot
475	240	9	Very Hot
500	250	10	Extremely Hot

Any broiling recipes can be used with the grill of the oven, but beware of high-temperature grills.

DATE			